# COPING WITH STRESS AND BURNOUT AS A VETERINARIAN

## An Evidence-Based Solution to Increase Wellbeing

## DR NADINE HAMILTON

Foreword by Emeritus Professor Trevor Heath OAM

**AUSTRALIAN**ACADEMIC**PRESS**

First published 2019 by:
Australian Academic Press Group Pty. Ltd.
Samford Valley QLD, Australia
www.australianacademicpress.com.au

A catalogue record for this book is available from the National Library of Australia

Coping with Stress and Burnout as a Veterinarian
ISBN 9781925644197    (paperback)

**Disclaimer**
Every effort has been made in preparing this work to provide information based on accepted standards and practice at the time of publication. The publisher and author, however, make no warranties of any kind of psychological outcome relating to use of this work and disclaim all responsibility or liability for direct or consequential damages resulting from any use of the material contained in this work.

Publisher & Editor: Stephen May
Cover design: Luke Harris, Working Type Studio
Typesetting: Australian Academic Press
Printing: Lightning Source

"Finally a practical self-help book aimed specifically at the veterinary profession written by a psychologist. Easy to read and with lots of practical advice it gives positive advice and the tools to traverse the corrugated road of professional life. It is perfect for the help-seeking profession we need to become."

**Dr Brian McErlean**
**Trustee, AVA Benevolent Fund and Veterinary Suicide Prevention Advocate**

"Dr Hamilton has noticed a problem in a professional body and is finding solutions to it. Being a veterinary clinician is stressful, no doubt and this book provides techniques to help manage stress which may be unique to the veterinary profession. Being a veterinary clinician is also a wonderful job therefore doing everything we can to alleviate the negatives is a win for me, therefore, this book is a win for me."

**Dr Alejandra Arbe**
**Small Animal Veterinarian, Researcher, The University of Adelaide**

"Never before in my veterinary career have I come across someone so passionate about making a difference. Not to their own lives or even that of loved ones they know — but to a profession as a whole. Nadine's determination to make a positive impact within the veterinary industry is palpable. Thank you Nadine, for recognising and building awareness around such an important issue. I highly recommend this book, it may just save a life one day."

**Dr Andy Pieris**
**Owner, Casuarina Seaside Vet**

"This book is a much-needed resource for veterinary professionals and comes from Dr Nadine Hamilton's solid doctoral research. In my opinion, this program is a great step forward to addressing mental health issues for veterinary professionals — to assist them take control of their wellbeing with evidence-based strategies."

*Merilyn Waterhouse*
*Psychologist*


"Dr Hamilton's book provides valuable insight into a sadly under-appreciated issue within our profession. It discusses not only influences on the mental health of veterinarians, but also strategies that can be utilised to assist with dealing with these. I'd recommend it wholeheartedly for all veterinarians and those that care for them."

*Dr Scott Campbell*
*Partner, Ipswich Vet Group*


"It is almost an unspoken rule or even a general acceptance that stress and burnout are just a fact of life if you are a veterinarian. It doesn't have to be that way. This book covers the background research explaining the root of the problem then the practical solutions and strategies for intervention all of which have been proven to make a significant difference in reducing stress, anxiety, and depression. The content of this easy-to-read resource is invaluable and the book should be on the reading list of those that are already a part of or considering entering the veterinary profession. Thank you Nadine for your incredible drive and passion that brought this book together. I believe it will make a difference, help veterinarians have successful and fulfilling careers and also most importantly save the lives of our dear colleagues."

*Dr Gerardo Poli*
*Hospital Director, Animal Emergency Service*

"As a clinical psychotherapist with over 30 years working with high performer medical professionals, I can say that Dr Nadine Hamilton has a deep understanding of the stresses, conflicts, and unique challenges causing anxiety, depression, burnout, and suicide in veterinarians today. She brings the results of her doctoral research and outlines a program veterinarians can use immediately to make a difference in their own life and that of the pets and the pet owners they care for. Dr Hamilton also addresses the need to reduce the stigma of getting help. She makes it clear when veterinarians need to go beyond what they can do on their own and when to reach out for professional help. I highly recommend this book to veterinarians and to the educators and mental health professionals who work with them."

*Dr Fern Kazlow*
*Clinical Psychotherapist, New York, Founder of The No Doubt Zone*

# Dedication

This book is dedicated to my cousin Andrew, whose suicide rocked our world but was the foundation for my work in suicide prevention.

It is dedicated to the many animals who I have been blessed to have in my life, who have instilled in me the feeling of unconditional love, and help to make the world a much better place.

It is also dedicated to all the veterinary professionals who have given, and continue to give, their all to help our beautiful animals.

And last, but certainly not least, to those veterinary professionals who paid the ultimate price by choosing to end their suffering. You will not be forgotten.

# Contents

## SECTION THREE — WHAT CAN HELP

# Acknowledgements

Many people assisted me in the preparation, conduct, and completion of the research that led to this book, and their assistance has been greatly appreciated.

To my incredible family for believing in me and supporting me every step of the way. To my best friend and husband Kirk for your patience, contributions, brainstorming, and support — not only during the research process, but continually throughout all my crazy ideas and 'moments' when I questioned things and felt like I was getting nowhere. You are my rock and biggest supporter and I am so grateful to have you by my side — I love you. To my amazing daughters, Cheyenne and Jaimie, who have often had to put up with a grumpy, stressed-out mum trying to put together my work and research. You are my angels, my helpers, and my heart and soul. I love you both so much. Last, but not least, Mum, Dad, Anita, and Rianna. You have all supported me in your own way and kept me motivated, and never seem to doubt my abilities to pull it all together and complete my work. I love you.

To my doctoral supervisors from the University of Southern Queensland, Dr Peter McIlveen, Professor and Dr Jan Du Preez, Lecturer. You have been an integral part of this journey, and have helped to keep me calm and rational during some stressful moments! Now we get to do it all over again with the PhD! Thank you, Peter and Jan, for your continued support — I could not have done this without you.

To the wonderful veterinarians who graciously gave up their time and shared their wisdom and experiences with me in my EdD research. I am forever grateful for your support, and can only hope that in turn, this research project does so much more for you in return. Thank you.

Thank you to my publisher Stephen May and Australian Academic Press, for taking the chance and believing in me and my work, and helping me to get this much-needed book to those who need it. Thank you.

I need to thank James Van Praagh for some special insights during a private session in 2016. Thank you, your words were like an epiphany to me and were the start of something amazing — the Love Your Pet Love Your Vet campaign! Thank you — without you, this may not have happened.

Thank you to my business and marketing mentor, Sue Painter, for your guidance and nudges to get this book written and published! Not to mention being the creative brains behind the Love Your Pet Love Your Vet campaign (where do you get your amazing ideas?).

I am also grateful to Emeritus Professor Trevor Heath OAM, for his continued support of my research and work — and for graciously accepting my offer to write the Foreword in this book. Thank you, Trevor, for everything you have done for me and the veterinary profession — you truly are a legend.

Lastly, I would like to acknowledge everyone who has supported me since finalising my EdD, and continued to be my cheer squad as we step into new adventures to create a much-needed paradigm shift for the veterinary profession. Thank you all.

Dr Nadine Hamilton is a psychologist who helps veterinary professionals get on top of stress and psychological fatigue to avoid burnout and suicide. She also works with practice managers and owners to increase wellbeing, productivity, and retention in the workplace.

Dr Hamilton has successfully completed doctoral research into veterinarian wellbeing, and commenced PhD studies in 2018 to further her research into stress, burnout, and suicide within the veterinary profession. She is the proud founder of *Love Your Pet Love Your Vet*, a not-for-profit charity raising awareness about the issues within the veterinary industry, and reducing stigma in veterinary professionals seeking help. Her campaign, supported by Royal Canin, has reached people and organisations around the world, and is leading the way in addressing veterinary suicide.

For more information, you can visit Dr Hamilton's websites at:

- Positive Psych Solutions — www.positivepsychsolutions.com.au
- Love Your Pet Love Your Vet — www.loveyourpetloveyourvet.com.au

A few years ago, I was asked to examine a doctoral thesis on applying the principles of psychology to mental ill-health in veterinarians. This was timely, for it seemed that veterinarians were increasingly becoming afflicted with such problems, and a distressing number apparently saw no solution beyond ending their lives.

As I reflected on the issue, I thought of the experience of the daughter of a friend of mine, Felicia, a smart, compassionate and committed veterinarian in her mid-twenties who was chuffed when she found a position in a suburban practice soon after she graduated. Several years later, she seemed disillusioned and often distressed; far from the positive, chirpy girl who said that she 'loved' animals and who was prepared to sacrifice so much during her school years to gain the score needed to gain entry to a veterinary school.

I knew she had worked hard during the five years of her veterinary course, and obviously looked forward to a career helping animals and their owners. But she soon found that her hopes were a bit idealistic. This became clear when she put a huge amount of time and emotional effort into treating a family pet only to find that the owners were dismissive, even critical, of her efforts. Furthermore, some clients would take exception to the cost, overlooking the fact that most health costs of other family members were borne by governments or other agencies.

Matters of cost were frequent causes of her despondency, especially when she had the will and the skill to treat a sick or injured pet, but the owners claimed an inability to pay, and even worse, asked that the animal be killed. Although the verb 'to kill' was usually disguised by euphemisms ('to put down' ... ), the emotional effect was the same, and cumulative. Overall, she felt that her career was not bringing the satisfaction that she had hoped for. Those feelings were coloured by another major concern: a low level of reward. Although not overly concerned about material things, Felicia was often reminded that her friends in other professions were being paid more for less work, less responsibility, and after a shorter and less demanding course. That, coupled with the demands of the workplace and a feeling that her best efforts were not being appreciated, were causing her to question her career path, despite still 'loving' animals, and being keen to help them.

All of these factors were having an adverse effect on her mental health, and she did not know what to do about it. She said that she often wondered whether her personality had in some way contributed to the way she was feeling. She'd always focussed on doing her best at whatever she did, and it was that drive that enabled her to achieve the score necessary to get into Veterinary School. But as a veterinarian she often felt thwarted, frustrated and disillusioned because other factors such as time, facilities or the owner's ability or willingness to pay prevented her from doing what she knew she could do for her patients. And these feelings were magnified if she was criticised or otherwise treated badly.

When Felicia sought out my counsel on her situation she recalled stories told by her grandfather Ramsay, of a very different time. Ramsay had been a veterinary surgeon in a country town for almost 50 years. He had often commented on how his clients expressed appreciation for his efforts, even when they did not work out well. Usually working alone, he apparently treated a wide variety of animals under many different conditions, and often at antisocial hours. But he said that he relished the role; he made an adequate income, and felt that he was appreciated and respected in his community. Even after decades in his practice he apparently had no wish to do anything else than work as a veterinarian and had found retirement somewhat difficult.

When Ramsay contemplated studying veterinary science there were no quotas on entry; all those who had completed requisite subjects at grade 12 could enrol. The numbers were small and those who sought a place seemed to do so because they enjoyed working with animals, mainly farm animals including working dogs. Almost all were male. Though compassionate, most of Ramsay's colleagues apparently did not have a strong emotional attachment for animals. That 'love' for animals among veterinarians became much more evident in later years, and seemed to coincide with the move in society for animals to be seen as integral parts of family units. About the same time as these changes occurred, the number of applicants for veterinary courses increased dramatically, and universities were forced to impose quotas on entry. As a result, only a minority of applicants could be offered a place. These included many who had (a) been driven by a 'love' for animals for most of their lives, and (b) been prepared to commit themselves to the hard work needed to gain a place in a quota.

As she thought about her situation, Felicia realised that the veterinary profession of which she was a part was vastly different from that of her grandfather's generation. And the members of her generation were subject to additional pressures to which some of them were especially susceptible, and this had adverse effects on their mental health.

It is impossible to know exactly how many other vets are out there experiencing the same concerns as Felicia. One reason for this uncertainty is that many, perhaps a majority, of those affected do not reveal that they are hurting. This may be because they fear they will be stigmatised, although this could be diminishing as more high-profile individuals discuss their mental health issues in public forums. But such evidence as is available indicates clearly that this is a problem of significant and extremely worrying magnitude among veterinarians.

Which brings me back to that thesis I was asked to examine. It was refreshing to find that a highly qualified and experienced psychologist was focusing on developing ways to help veterinarians. As I found when I read the thesis, she had applied great expertise and insight to the issue — and thoroughly deserved her doctorate.

That psychologist was of course the author of this book, Nadine Hamilton. Since her thesis she has worked hard and effectively to increase community awareness of mental ill-health among veterinarians, and to make available credible, psychologically-based approaches to improving the health and life of those veterinarians. The development of this book is a central part of a broad-based strategy, and I am delighted to be associated with it.

Nadine's contributions as set out in the content of this book and her unique wellbeing program for veterinarians as well as via her professional psychology practice place her at the forefront of a wave of professional targeted help for the veterinary profession. I'm hugely impressed, and recommend this book in the strongest terms.

**Emeritus Professor Trevor Heath OAM**

For as long as I can remember I have loved animals and as a child all I wanted to do was grow up and become a vet. When I was born (back in the United Kingdom quite a few decades ago), my parents owned a Rough Collie called 'Shane'. He was an amazing and beautiful dog and had a very long and happy life. My nana and poppa looked after him when we emigrated to New Zealand, and we missed him like crazy. However, when he sadly passed away at a very old age, my dad swore he would never get another dog — and he never has. He felt the pain of losing a beloved family member was too much and didn't want to go through that again. I, on the other hand, am a different kettle of fish — I love having animals around me and find the years of love and joy outweigh the grief when we lose them. To this day, I credit Shane for my love of animals.

My yearning to become a vet changed one day however when I took my precious guinea pig 'Pepi' to the vet, who just happened to be the dad of one of my school friends. I clearly remember sitting in the waiting room and realising I could never operate on an animal (way too queasy for that!), nor could I put one to sleep. I had an inkling that there was something about performing euthanasia that wasn't so good. Maybe I wouldn't become a vet after all. Instead, I went on to fail every subject in my high school exams by talking too much (it's actually documented in my school reports!). Perhaps it was due to undiagnosed ADD or I just didn't relate to the 'lecture-and-learn' style of teaching. In any case, at 15 years of age my parents gave me an ultimatum — if I found myself a job I could leave school, otherwise I would have to go back and repeat that year. I hated school, so I became a high-school dropout and found myself my first job.

I remember riding the bus to work one day to my new job as a mailroom clerk in Auckland as we drove past an educational facility. I told myself that I would never go to university because I had failed high school. As it turns out, I was wrong again about my future. (Never discount someone who has fierce determination and a stack of optimism — my name means 'hope', so it seems I've always been destined to be optimistic!)

My parents and I left New Zealand and returned to the UK when I was 16. We stayed for around four months while I ventured into dental nursing, which I really didn't enjoy (remember me mentioning the queasy bit before?), before emigrating to Australia just after I turned 17. I tried to find work as a vet nurse without success and ended up returning to dental nursing before eventually working in administrative jobs. I was not that happy about my work though. I felt like something was missing, and that I hadn't yet found my calling.

By chance a book I read from the library I often frequented finally helped me name what it was I was interested in — psychology. Despite being uncertain as to my success about being accepted into university (bearing in mind I was a high-school dropout), I applied as a mature-age student and was accepted! My excitement at becoming a psychology student was somewhat short-lived, when we received news that one of my beloved cousins, Andrew, had committed suicide back in the UK. It had a lasting impact. While discussing my future psychology career at a residential school for university not long after this, I talked about working with people who were suicidal. I was told that as I was only at the start of my psychology training I would probably change my mind numerous times before I began practising. As things turned out, that was right — initially. I ended up focusing on organisational psychology and pursued further training and qualifications, but still didn't feel like I had found my true calling.

Then one day I had an appointment with a locum at my local vet clinic.

We got to talking about what kind of work I did, and when I mentioned I was a psychologist she made me aware of the statistics of vet suicide. I was stunned. Why did this profession which I had admired for so long have such a disturbing rate of the ultimate self-harm and how could one help? Then I realised that my passion for animals and the veterinary industry now had an outlet entirely compatible with my personal desire to work with people who were suicidal.

For six-and-a-half years I conducted doctoral research into veterinarian wellbeing to investigate existing studies which reported the alarming rate of suicide. I wanted to not only replicate these findings — but do something proactive about it.

My Doctor of Education studies were successfully completed in 2016, and since then I have continued to work within the veterinary industry to raise awareness and educate others about the statistics. In early-2017 I founded *Love Your Pet Love Your Vet*, a global campaign with the backing of pet food giant Royal Canin to reduce the stigma of seeking help for vets, to raise awareness within the community of the high burnout and suicide in the profession, and to provide practical support. I also found time to write this book, based on the research I had read and conducted and the vets I had worked with in my private psychology practice.

If you are already working within the veterinary industry or considering doing so, then I'm sure the information in this book will come as no surprise to you — that veterinarians are four times more likely to commit suicide than the general community, and twice as likely as other health care professionals. However, this book is a little bit different to most others as illustrated in its arrangement into four distinct sections. As well as describing the clear mental health **challenge** to the veterinary profession, I also look at what the **reality** of being a vet is. This in turn can tell us something about **what can help** vets in distress through an examination of four key psychological approaches to personal wellbeing. In the final section of the book I present a self-help version of a practical psycho-educational **intervention** called the *Coping and Wellbeing Program for Veterinary Professionals* which provides coping tools to help you deal better with stress, anxiety, and depression.

I hope this book can help any vet seeking some support and understanding of their unique work life, a colleague you notice is struggling, a student starting out in the profession, or maybe a vet school lecturer interested in ensuring their students are given a fully rounded education. My hope also is that any vet who feels they are struggling seeks professional help early. Talking with a psychologist in private is a positive and strong first step toward a better life for yourself, and those around you.

# SECTION ONE

# The Challenge

# Chapter 1

# The 'Dark Side' of
# the Veterinary Profession

When you ask a veterinarian about their job most will answer along the lines that it is a rewarding, but challenging and demanding career. They might also say that to be successful you must have a passion for or a clinical interest in animals, have great interpersonal skills and possess a strong work ethic. Many vets will happily recount a childhood passion for animals or a childhood pet that led them to eventually pursuing a career as a vet.

Not surprisingly then, many people have the perception that being a vet is a wonderful job because you get to play with kittens and puppies all day long. There is also a perception that becoming a vet means you will be very well paid. Certainly, most pet owners' experiences with vet bills lead them to believe that someone is making a good living.

Sadly, these assumptions are not the stuff of reality. While it can be a rewarding and satisfying career, there is also a 'dark side' to the profession for the unwary.

## The Problem

Veterinarians have long been considered the guardians of animal welfare and health. In earlier times, they were required to work in professional isolation at all times of the day and night and expected to work with all species of animals. Today they work in an ever more diverse environment and specialist areas. The effects of working long hours, performing euthanasia on animals, emotional pressure, financial issues, unrealistic expectations, and dealing with distressed clients place considerable stress on both the vet themselves and their families at home.

Failure to cope with stress can lead to emotional problems such as depression and suicide, physical problems such as psoriasis and being vulnerable to infection, and behavioural issues such as irritability and anger. Working the unsocial and long hours that are generally required, juggling the emotional involvement with patients but also being able to detach from them emotionally, as well as the need to be self-critical but balancing this with the ability not to be too critical, can be a risk factor to the onset of depression. With a lot of vets tending to be perfectionists, there is also the risk of many practitioners being workaholics without strong support systems. This can lead to a tendency for vets to hide things that are bothering them and continue to push on, ignoring their symptoms.

It may not come as any surprise then that the mental health of vets is showing serious signs of sickness.

Within Australia a veterinarian will commit suicide approximately every 12 weeks, In the period from 1990 to 2002, 11 vets in Victoria and Western Australia committed suicide. The rates of suicide for vets in Victoria and Western Australia are estimated to be 3.8 times and 4.0 times respectively, the age-standardised rate for suicide in the adult populations of their respective states. Further, it was reported that for two states within Australia, vets had a suicide rate of 45 per 100,000-person-years, which is roughly four times the general population rate within these two states. The former coordinator of the OneLife Suicide Prevention Project for the Western Australian division of the Australian Veterinary Association (AVA), Dr Brian McErlean, reported the following statistics for vets within Australia, with a comparison to the general population figures provided in brackets:

- Depression — mild to severe = 25% (20%).

- Depression — extremely severe = 3.9% (2%).

- Work-related burnout = 35.8% (20%).

McErlean also states that the suicide risk for vets begins at graduation and remains throughout the rest of the life span. This is particularly prevalent in vets who graduate and relocate to a remote location for work, experiencing isolation and relationship breakdowns — which are high-risk factors for severe depression in vets. Further he reports, depression can lead to substance abuse, which is subsequently exacerbated by vets having 24/7 access to drugs.

In the United Kingdom, rates of suicide have been reported at least three times the general population rate, with the most common methods used being firearms and self-poisoning. In the five-years from 1994 to 1998, pharmacists, farmers, physicians, and dentists had up to twice the expected rate of suicide as the general population (using the proportional mortality ratio, or PMR), with the highest rate attributed to vets at more than three times the PMR.

Statistics reported from England and Wales found that for the period 1979 to 1990, 35 out of 383 veterinarian deaths were attributed to suicide. Gender differences were reported whereby one in every four female deaths was the result of suicide. For the period 1991 to 2000, there was reportedly approximately one suicide for every 11 deaths in male vets, and one in every six deaths for female vets. In addition to this, there were investigations into the characteristics of the electoral ward of the usual residence of deceased individuals, with linked data from death certificates. It was stated that relative to death from natural causes, the risk of suicide among 16 to 44-year old male vets, 45 to 64-year old male vets, and 16 to 64-year old female vets, is increased by 4.6, 5.6, and 7.6 times respectively, when compared to people within the general population that have similar demographical characteristics.

In the United States, recent research by the Centers for Disease Control and Prevention's National Institute for Occupational Safety and Health concluded that when compared to the general population in the United States, female veterinarians were 3.5 times as likely and male veterinarians were 2.1 times as likely to commit suicide.

Similar statistics have also been reported in New Zealand, with the New Zealand Veterinary Association stating that the vet profession worldwide is one of the leading professions in suicide rates.

In 2012, the Canadian Veterinary Medical Association reported that 19 per cent of member respondents to a survey had seriously thought about suicide, with 9 per cent having previously made an attempt on their life. Twenty-seven per cent reported that they took anti-depressants.

While the total number of vets as an occupation is relatively small and the actual number of suicides within this profession is low, an alarming 43% of veterinarian deaths is due to suicide with 41.8 to 52.6 veterinarians per 100,000 worldwide ending their life through suicide. It is clear that when compared with the general population and other occupations, vets are at a significantly higher risk of suicide. Even the most qualified and passionate vets are at risk.

## Why do so many vets contemplate suicide?

Although the reasons for the higher suicide risk are not immediately clear, a number of likely factors have been identified. These include:

- The coping styles and personality traits of individuals applying to veterinary school.

- Having the knowledge of which doses and drugs are likely to cause death by intentional self-poisoning, as well as having ready access to these medicines.

- Experiencing both professional and social isolation.

- Working within a 'culture of death' (such as an acceptance of slaughter and animal euthanasia).

- High levels of student debt from veterinary school.

- Dealing with the increasing expectations of clients.

- Fearing the stigma involved with seeking help.

- Working long hours.

There is without a doubt a significant emotional cost to working as a vet, and euthanasia of companion animals is quite a significant contributing factor. Euthanasia can be highly distressing for pet owners, and while their emotional reactions are considered 'normal' in these circumstances, the vet and vet nurses are expected to remain professionally objective during the process of euthanasia, despite what they themselves may also be feeling. To what extent the actual process of euthanising a pet in this context impacts upon vets and vet nurses is not well-researched.

Some studies suggest that vets may commit suicide because they are more exposed to the practice of euthanasia, and therefore may have different attitudes towards life and death. They may experience conflict between their values of wanting to preserve the life of animals and being unable to successfully treat these animals for whatever reason. This conflict could be responsible for vets lowering any reservations they have with suicide being a solution to their own problems — providing a self-justification for them to take their own life. Seeing euthanasia as an end to pain and suffering can often reinforce to the vet who is suffering that this is an option they can choose to end their own pain and suffering. Perhaps adding to this risk, vets have knowledge of, and ready access to, medicines for self-poisoning, and are also under less supervision than doctors with their use of medicines.

UK-based veterinarian researcher David Bartram spent several years conducting mental-health research within the veterinary profession to aid in the wellbeing of individual vets, as well as examining the impact that vet mental ill-health could have on the welfare of animals under their care, and gaining insight into suicidal influences.

According to Bartram, a major factor impacting veterinarian suicide is depression, and many vets themselves may have a predisposition that can lead to depression. When compared to the general population, vets are more likely to appear in the moderate, severe, and very severe ranges for symptoms of depression. Their suicide risk is higher than medical doctors and dentists, and having access to lethal medication as a means of suicide can translate thoughts of suicide into actual behaviour. Risk factors for suicide also include undesirable life events, certain personality traits, major chronic difficulties, alcohol and drug abuse, and depression.

Other factors having a potential impact on suicide within the veterinary profession include stress, working long hours, working on-call and after-hours, expectations of clients, relationships with peers, clients, and managers, dealing with difficult clients, unexpected clinical outcomes, emotional exhaustion, inadequate professional support, lack of resources, personal finances, making professional mistakes, and the possibility of litigation or client complaints.

The Centre for Suicide Research at Oxford University conducted research into the significantly elevated rates of vet suicide in Australia, Belgium, Norway, the United Kingdom, and the United States. The results of their research suggest again a very real link between the veterinary profession and the high risk of suicide. They report that possible explanations for this high suicide rate are:

- individuals accepted into veterinary school have traits which may include conscientiousness, perfectionism, neurosis, and being high achievers (some admission procedures for veterinary degrees seem to only favour those who are high achievers);

- social isolation of solo practitioners; working in an environment that often requires long hours with potentially little support from managers; high psychological demands and high expectations from clients;

- ready access to medications and knowledge of how to use them;

- exposure to colleagues' suicides which could result in copycat suicides; and

- acceptance of euthanasia as a philosophical way of alleviating suffering.

Furthermore, factors such as overwork, substance abuse, compassion fatigue, burnout, relationship distress, and depression are all potential factors contributing to psychological distress.

In New Zealand, a survey was developed to try and identify self-reported levels of depression and stress in vets, the sources of stress within their profession, and what forms of social support were used. The results showed that younger vets were more likely to experience higher levels of stress than older vets, women experienced more depression and work-related stress than men, and those working in small animal and/or mixed practices reported more depression and stress than did those in other fields of veterinary work. Sources of stress were highlighted as client expectations, hours worked, and unexpected outcomes. Additionally, the study also identified that vets were also stressed by finances, personal relationships, relationships with managers, peers, and clients, lack of resources, performing euthanasia, work-life balance, health, concerns relating to their career path, their expectations of themselves, and requirements to keep technical skills and knowledge updated.

Other research has found stressors for vets also include managing adverse events, working in teams, giving bad news, interacting with difficult clients, balancing home/work life, and the strongest — dealing with ethical dilemmas. Additionally, working in an animal shelter, dealing with animal cruelty, dealing with the public, the intensity and frequency of euthanasia, conflict within the workplace, and the constant influx of animals, are also contributing factors to vet stress.

While some stress can be necessary for optimal performance (eustress), stress that is not managed effectively (distress) can have negative repercussions such as depression, anxiety, substance abuse, burnout, relationship issues, a negative work/home life environment, and suicide. Further, links between suicide and compassion fatigue, hours worked, workplace relationships, moral stress, and difficult life events are all contributing factors. There have also been reports that students of veterinary medicine found their continued exposure to euthanasia was related to a sense of fearlessness about death.

Few studies to date however, have specifically researched mental health difficulties and suicidal behaviour, although there are indications that the vets at greatest risk are females and young vets, with these individuals at higher risk of job dissatisfaction, mental health difficulties, and suicidal thoughts. There is a clear age-related trend with younger vets being more likely than their older counterparts to be anxious, depressed, or distressed. However, research has found that vets who graduated earlier, or who had been practising in a job for a long period of time, were less likely to report symptoms of depression, distress, and anxiety. Interestingly, vets who graduated prior to 1970 were found less likely to experience psychological distress than those who graduated after 1990. While it is quite common for vets to experience poor psychological health, the levels of distress, depression, and anxiety were found similar to other professional or managerial positions in the United Kingdom. It was also found that recent graduates and those working long hours had the worst psychological health.

Despite thoughts that may suggest otherwise, individuals from high socioeconomic classes, professionals, and those who are very high functioning, can experience events such as relational crises, depression, anxiety, and life events, which can create pathways to suicidal behaviours and thoughts. When these events occur — and mental health issues become problematic — feelings of helplessness, hopelessness, and worthlessness may be experienced, leaving the individual feeling immeasurable psychological pain. Once a person has taken extreme measures and completed suicide, the effects are far-reaching — that is, it affects friends, family, teachers, co-workers, counsellors, and acquaintances, to the extent that often these individuals may experience reactions that are severely emotional for many years after the suicide. Not to mention the loss of the intellectual gifts and talents of the individual who has taken their own life. It is fair to say that mental illness and suicide does not discriminate — sadly, it has the potential to affect anyone.

A psychological theory termed the 'stress-diathesis model' suggests that an individual's stressful life events, vulnerability, or predisposition results in suicidal behaviour. Such vulnerability has an influence on how the person interprets, perceives, and reacts to adverse life events, and is a product of previous life events, psychobiological factors, and genetic predisposition. This model is consistent with the 'cry of pain' model of suicidal behaviour identified by psychologists Williams and Pollock, which suggests that suicidal behaviour is the cry, or response, to situations an individual finds stressful, and where they may feel defeated, humiliated, trapped, or needing to escape. Psychological variables such as the ability to think about the future positively, as well as problem-solving abilities, can affect such judgements.

Despite the evidence of challenges to the mental health and wellbeing facing vets, seeking help is not often the first instinct. In my own research and practice, I have found that a lot of vets have such high levels of pride and intelligence along with high achieving personalities they believe they should be able to effectively deal with any problem that comes their way — without seeking the help of anyone else. Sadly, this leads to many vets suffering in silence unnecessarily, which then has a flow-on effect to their colleagues, clients, families, and friends.

# What do we do to help vets at risk?

One innovative approach to tackle high stress and the ever threat of suicidality is to be found in the profession of career counselling. As will be covered later in Chapter 5, the theory of career construction counselling is highly applicable to the veterinary profession due to certain unique aspects of a vet's daily work. Sadly, due to the unpleasant things those in the veterinary profession have to deal with, not all vets will choose to remain working when facing significant psychological distress. It is therefore equally important for aspiring and prospective vets to have a thorough understanding of the demands of working in the industry, and as such, it could be beneficial to work with a career professional using career construction counselling prior to embarking on this journey.

Career counsellors can also have an impact on being able to assist vets who may be battling with suicidal ideation as, given the right tools and support, they are uniquely positioned to assess their clients for suicidal ideation due to their less-stigmatised position. By listening to their clients and asking them about suicide, career counsellors can gain knowledge of whether they are experiencing transitory or passive ideation, or whether their suicidal ideas are more imminent or serious. This may enable career counsellors to become more confident and competent in directly asking their client about their suicidality, or conducting in-depth assessments, or even having a discussion with their client that may alleviate the stigma surrounding suicide.

Due to the belief that there is a strong connection between suicidality and employment, it is possible that many individuals struggling with issues relating to work are experiencing depression, anxiety, isolation, or substance misuse — all of which have associated risk factors with suicidal ideation. Additionally, this connection also emphasises a disruption in employment, learning disabilities, socioeconomic status, sudden unemployment, interpersonal conflicts, difficulties at work, and occupational stress.

Clearly, there is also a need for professional veterinary bodies to consider the provision of training for vets in dealing with work-related distress, depression, and anxiety and indeed it has been suggested in the past that cognitive-behavioural (CBT) based therapies are a potential intervention. Yet CBT can only go so far. Present manualised approaches for conditions such as adult depression do not consider the specifics of a workday faced by a busy vet.

The importance of emotion-focused and problem-focused strategies alongside CBT is suggested as an important next step in assisting vets to cope with the stressors of their work. The veterinary profession should be encouraged to adopt effective intervention strategies using these approaches. Given the multiple factors identified as contributing to suicidal behaviour, teaching vets more effective behavioural and cognitive coping strategies forms part of a holistic approach to suicide prevention and early intervention for psychological distress.

## Developing an Effective Psychological Intervention for Veterinary Professionals

Research has shown that a person's coping strategies to deal with stress can cover the range from dangerously self-destructive such as drug and alcohol abuse to highly effective evidence-based strategies stemming from applied psychology such as mindfulness and positive psychology. Yet research specific to the veterinary profession has been thin on the ground. Little has been done to provide well-researched, appropriate, and adequate intervention strategies for vets other than the provision of telephone support, crisis lines, and limited cognitive behavioural therapy strategies.

If we are to progress research into vet wellbeing and attempt to find effective solutions that can help prepare and empower those within the profession to deal with the realities of working as a vet, we need to delve deeper into the real-life issues that are hindering wellbeing. Dealing with 'band-aid' solutions or 'tip of the iceberg' situations is extremely unlikely to generate significant, lasting, psychological change. We need to get to the core or root of the problem and deal with these issues (as uncomfortable as this may be for some people) if we want things to change effectively. This concern is not going away and can no longer be hidden under the table with an 'all is well' attitude.

The reality is that whether we acknowledge the sad, hurtful, and even traumatic things that have happened in our lives or not, it doesn't change the reality of what happened. The more you avoid dealing with them, the bigger and more powerful they can seem. When you cano safely acknowledge and accept the reality that they happened, and work through these issues with someone qualified to help you through this, real change can occur. This is where I strongly advocate for support from an appropriatly qualified and experienced professional (such as a psychologist and/or psychiatrist) to help distressed vets work through their issues in a safe, supportive, and caring environment.

What is also needed are effective proven and beneficial programs being provided to vets to assist them in dealing with the everyday demands of their profession — a psychological toolbox of resources they can refer to when required. That's why the *Coping and Wellbeing Program for Veterinary Professionals* (included in Section 4 of this book) was developed for both guided intervention and self-help support. Built from evidence-based theory and practice, the program is a unique professional development and psycho-educational intervention. It educates vets on how to develop protective attitudes, enhance wellbeing, and subsequently increase their coping skills.

Using a range of strategies that are relatively straightforward and easy to implement the program assists participants in dealing with unhelpful thoughts, feelings, and behaviours, as well as stress-management strategies, time-management skills, communication and assertiveness skills, relaxation strategies, goal setting, and wellbeing recommendations. Overall, the program provides for a holistic approach to wellbeing by not only focusing on tackling the psychological ill-health considerations to be discussed throughout this book, but also offering proactive solutions for those who may not currently be experiencing symptoms of distress, but who desire to maintain their current levels of wellbeing.

Early outcome research on the program's effectiveness has shown a significant decrease in symptoms of depression, anxiety, stress, and negative affect — all of which are contributing factors to psychological wellbeing. Following participation in the program, vets also indicated they were better able to cope with the demands of their everyday lives once they had learnt the strategies taught, and they felt better about themselves.

It is hoped that access to an expanded group version of the program will be made available for both vets in training and those working in organisations and practices to enhance and sustain wellbeing. If you would like to attend a group workshop based on the program or are interested in arranging a workshop for your organisation, you can find more details of the program at www.positivepsychsolutions.com.au.

Before we get to Section 4 and the program, it is useful to explore the experience of being a veterinarian and the range of strategies and coping tools to reduce psychological distress available to the profession. Chapter 2 examines the profession today and the ways in which being a vet comes with its own unique stressors and risks that impact on wellbeing as well as looking at the strengths of a 'successful' vet and the support mechanisms currently available.

# SECTION TWO

# The Reality

# Being a Veterinarian

There have been substantive changes to the veterinary profession in both training and practice over the past 30 years. Most notably, there has been a massive gender shift from it being seen traditionally as a male occupation. It is estimated that the percentage of females working in the veterinary profession increased from 15% in 1981 to 46% in 2006. Today, nearly two-thirds of graduates are women. It is also now common among vets to have poor psychological health, with females fairing worse than males. It has also been found that female veterinarians who had never been pregnant or had children, had worse mental health than those who had two or more children. For both men and women stress, depression, and burnout have all been reported as a result of organisational, personal, and interpersonal factors.

Additionally, there has also been a decrease in income levels and status for the profession when compared to other occupations. Some influences affecting status, in particular, have been reported as linked to an individual's ability to recognise changing expectations with clients and the community, as well as the challenge of self-promotion within the communities a vet serves.

Noted veterinary researcher Emeritus Professor Trevor Heath has documented changes over vet's initial career experiences over the last five decades, which include the following:

- An increase in the percentage of female graduates.

- Changes from government services to private practice employment.

- An increase in the number of vets within the workplace.

- Decreases in after-hours duty and work hours.

- An increase in emphasis on lifestyle.

- Caseload changes with more cats/dogs and fewer farm animals.

- An increase and change in levels of support.

- A decrease in the breadth of competence expected at graduation.

- An increase in bureaucratic red tape, and a decrease in respect from clients.

- Changes and recent improvements in the overall attitude to the first year as vets.

- Changes and improvements in attitudes to being a vet and completing a degree.

- Changes in the work carried out as a vet.

- A decrease in the percentage of vets serving rural industries.

- An increase in the percentage of small animal practice.

- Gender differences in type of work.

- A decrease in practice ownership.

- Differences in practice ownership between genders.

- A change in the location of work.

Heath further notes that most veterinary schools worldwide now include specific training in communication skills for students, reflecting the growing recognition of the importance of establishing and maintaining client relationships. It was not until the mid-1980s that explicit instruction in client communication was first provided as part of a veterinary school curriculum when it was introduced by The University of Queensland.

In response to these ongoing changes in the profession, the Australian Veterinary Association suggests as a core competency that vets now need the ability to adapt to advances in technology and changes of practice within their field. In some states within Australia it is now compulsory for vets to regularly update and refine their skills through professional development training, a change seen in most health professions these days. Yet practice skills training can only do so much to affect wellbeing outcomes for vets. Day-to-day working pressures, psychological and physical isolation, lack of support, and the requirements to remain up-to-date can all add up to leaving a vet feeling vulnerable and unable to cope.

An understanding of exactly how a vet's life and practice is impacted upon by issues both unique to the profession as well as applicable to general work and business provides the best chance to reduce the mental distress and restore wellbeing through targeted interventions. A variety of research studies have identified a range of impacts on vet wellbeing.

## Impacts on Vet Wellbeing

### Financial issues

*Income*

Low wages for vets remain an issue, compounded by the often-incorrect belief in the community that due to the high charge-out rates for services and treatment, vets must be very wealthy. Yet many vets report lower-than-expected incomes, considering the nature of their work and the amount of training they have undertaken to gain entry to the profession. For some vets, they may feel that after the costs of overheads, there is very little money to be made in the industry. For veterinary nurses in particular, there may be limited scope for advancement once they have already reached practice manager status, placing a ceiling on their earning capacity.

*Financial costs*

These include the costs of running a practice, such as purchasing and maintaining equipment, staff wages, rent, telephones, electricity, stationery, uniforms, equipment, medications, and the regulatory compliance costs of running a business in today's economy. The cost of repairing some equipment can be in the tens of thousands of dollars, and the cost of setting up a substantial new practice in some regions can run into millions. It is easy to see how quickly a practice's profit margins can reduce.

### Dealing with clients

One of the most significant wellbeing issues reported by vets is the stress they feel when dealing with difficult or emotionally distressed clients — the human owners, not the animals. Dealing with clients while they are in an emotional state is an obvious stressor, and this circumstance can occur often in a veterinary practice. Clients may become upset due to the distress or condition of their pet, be angry because they perceive treatment expenses are too high or because their animal cannot be saved, or become highly emotional in the case of euthanasia.

Having to deal with owners of animals that had been brought into emergency care by other people (such as an animal being hit by a car) is often problematical. Veterinary staff usually have to treat these cases as emergencies, frequently resulting in their pre-booked appointments having to wait while the emergency is attended to. This has a flow-on effect as often it can result in staff working through lunch breaks or working after-hours, limiting the time they would then be able to spend with their families at home. Such emergencies also place additional stress on the running of the practice, as other clients with scheduled appointments are then forced to wait for unknown amounts of time while the emergency is attended to.

Adding to this is the fact that often with emergency cases, once the animal has been successfully treated, the owner may come to the practice to claim and collect their pet not expecting to pay for the services and treatment their pet has received. There is an expectation from some clients that a vet will treat their animal for free, due to the nature of the job — 'vets love animals and will do anything for them'.

Some clients have further unrealistic expectations of their vet in terms of diagnosis and treatment, demanding instant diagnosis and complete resolution of the animal's condition in quick succession. For example, if an animal is treated for a papilloma and it regrows, the client may hold the vet responsible because of an unrealistic belief that such tumours will never return. Yet in medicine with humans, generally the doctor would not be accused of performing the initial excision incorrectly, rather the understanding is that the biological aspects of the disease in the first place always means it could return. Unfortunately, in veterinary medicine, it is all too likely the vet would be blamed for some perceived lack of care or skill.

### Unrealistic financial expectations from clients

Perhaps one of the most contentious issues in the veterinary industry that impacts on vet wellbeing as alluded to earlier is speaking with clients about money. This has been reported as being a major issue, as most vets come into their career in veterinary medicine to do their best for each patient, however, when financial issues become involved it can be heart-wrenching and very tricky, to say the least. This leaves the vet trying to weigh up the best interest of the animal, the demands of their business, and the financial circumstances of the client — resulting in the vet often being in a terrible dilemma. One example is a vet who was taken advantage of by a client who brought his pet in for treatment and left without paying a cent, then returned a few months later, expecting free treatment for another pet, and subsequently blamed the vet for being uncaring and heartless when she rightly refused!

Stress stemming from a client's reaction to treatment costs are multi-faceted. This includes the unrealistic expectations of what money can buy, 'fix' and treat. At one end of the spectrum is the general consensus that some pet owners believe money can fix anything, and as such, expect vets to 'work miracles' by completely curing their pet without question, even when it is evident the issues facing the animal are life-threatening and no amount of money will make a difference.

On the other end of the spectrum are those owners who do not believe they should have to pay for treatment. For example — if an animal was brought into the practice by a third party following an accident, and the owner does not expect to have to pay for the veterinary care that had taken place to treat the animal during the emergency.

An owner unable or unwilling to pay the required treatment costs for their animal may often result in the animal's unnecessary euthanasia — despite the treatment being able to potentially save the animal's life. In some cases, vets treat animals at their own expense to avoid this. It is not surprising then that many vets today support pet insurance, believing that if more owners had pet insurance, funds would be available to cover some if not all, costs of treatment — thus avoiding unnecessary euthanasia.

Another aspect of treatment costs is being able to provide treatment that is available and beneficial, but owners being ignorant or choosing not to be compliant, thus often resulting in unnecessary euthanasia.

There are also those rare clients who are difficult to deal with in general, and who may become angry because they have had to outlay money to have their pet treated when in their opinion this money could have been better spent on themselves.

### Client non-compliance

An issue many vets report as negatively affecting their wellbeing is related to the non-compliance of clients. There are many different circumstances where this applies. A common theme is when an owner wants to keep their pet alive no matter what, yet the vet believes the best interests of the animal are to euthanase it to treat it humanely and respectfully. Denial can also play a part when owners choose to not acknowledge their animal's situation, often resulting in the animal's prolonged suffering, and generally ending with euthanasia.

### Compassion fatigue

Common in the helping and healing professions is compassion fatigue, and the veterinary profession is certainly no exception. Compassion fatigue can be defined as a state of preoccupation and tension whereby the suffering of those being helped can extend to secondary traumatic stress for the helper. It is a state experienced by those helping distressed animals or humans. According to the Compassion Fatigue Awareness Project*, it can hurt when we care too much, and destructive behaviours can arise when the helpers do not focus on practising self-care — and instead place their focus on others.

Trying to remain compassionate to both animal and owner can be challenging at times, although this is prevalent particularly in times of trauma or end-of-life situations. Balancing the reality of quality of life for a pet, as well as understanding the close relationship many owners have with their pets and the human-animal bond about to be severed, requires some juggling. For some vets, this can be exceptionally difficult when they have

---

* http://www.compassionfatigue.org/

known the animal throughout its life span, and/or when they are particularly fond of the owners.

Other client interaction issues include:

- Communication — clients may be seen as rude, not knowing how to communicate in a clear, respectful way, or be difficult to understand due to language differences, as well as some clients expecting their vet to 'drop everything' to speak with them.

- Gender biases — there is mixed evidence as to the prevalence of gender bias in the profession, though it has been reported particularly from female vets. An example would be a client asking whether a female vet would hand off the care of the customer's pet to a male vet despite the female vet being more qualified and experienced than her male counterparts.

- Blame — vets are directly in the blame firing line when a client's beloved pet dies and may be accused of not treating the animal effectively or correctly. In cases where an angry outburst may result in a vet being told they are incompetent and did not do enough to save a pet, psychological damage may be inflicted that will not be undone even if the client apologises.

## Performing euthanasia

Long thought to be the biggest contributing factor to vet wellbeing, euthanasia of animals continues to be reported by vets as an unpleasant aspect of their job, even when it is in the best interests of the animal. It is of course a stressful aspect of veterinary medicine, especially when the euthanasia involves companion animals. However, it was not the sole factor, and not all vets feel it is the most significant factor. Some vets have noted that longevity in their career is somewhat of a protective factor against the negative effects of euthanasing an animal.

Reported explanations as to why performing euthanasia is distressing for vets include that the vet is inevitably ending an animal's life, and the bond that was shared between owner and animal is thus severed forever. Even when the euthanasia is necessary and there are no other options available, this task remains a difficult one for some vets. Performing euthanasia can also be distressing due to dealing with the owner's emotional and psychological state prior to, during, and after, the euthanasia has been performed. This is closely related to compassion fatigue as mentioned earlier. A vet must be able to relate to both the grieving client, as well as the suffering animal. According to some, the majority of vets believe veterinary schools should have more emphasis on the necessary communication skills to assist them in dealing with owners of animals that are terminally ill. Indeed, many vets are not adequately trained in how to deal with pet loss and client emotion, and even as recent as twenty years-or-so ago, many veterinary schools did not address factors concerning emotionally distressed clients, or issues around euthanasia — nor did they provide effective instruction in how to deal with pet owners who were grieving. How a vet views euthanasia can make a difference in the experience of the resultant grief, and whether they perceive euthanasia as something they physically do to a pet, or something they can give to a pet.

Another reason for finding euthanasia so distressing is in situations where it is deemed unnecessary — such as owners not being able to afford treatment. It also can apply to those working at facilities such as pounds, where many animals are euthanased due to apparent behavioural issues, or other reasons. Some vets also report that euthanasia can be made more difficult due to the species of animal they are dealing with. Some animals are easier to euthanase than others due to their physiology and size. With others, the procedure does not always result in instant death.

Additionally, euthanasia can be difficult due to the life span of animals generally being shorter than humans. This results in some vets knowing the animal and their owners throughout the animal's life span and developing their own bond with the animal (and occasionally their owners). I know this was the case when we had our beloved 'Caddy' put to sleep — our wonderful vet had treated Caddy since she was a puppy, so almost 16 years later it was quite difficult to say those final goodbyes. I vividly remember looking up at the vet nurse (who had also known Caddy for many years), who had tears streaming down her face as the euthanasia took place.

### Day-to-day stressors

Unfortunately for many vets, simply working in their profession will involve daily stressors capable of affecting their level of wellbeing. A major study of vet stress conducted back in 1999 showed that while levels of stress did not significantly vary between the type of work, gender, or number of people within the workplace, the levels of stress connected with general life events was inclined to decrease with age. It was also found that female vets reported feelings of depression more so than men and were more likely than men to feel stressed by the most demanding situations at work. However, females were not considerably more stressed than their male counterparts by a typical day at work or life in general. In addition, those working in large organisations were found to be more stressed than those in smaller organisations, and those working in small animal practice found the most demanding situation at work more stressful than those working in other fields.

Results also showed older vets were less stressed by hours worked, client communication, client expectations, unexpected outcomes, and lack of support from senior colleagues than were younger vets. Male vets were also less likely than females to report an increase in stress due to colleague and/or employer expectations, hours worked, communication with clients, resources, support from senior colleagues, expectations from clients, unexpected outcomes, and professional support. Further, vets in clinical practice appeared to experience lower stress levels from the expectations of their colleagues and employer, support from senior colleagues, and lack of resources, than those not working in clinical practice. However, they did report feeling more stress from dealing with unexpected outcomes and expectations from clients.

### Grief

Dealing with a client's grief, particularly during traumatic situations such as euthanasia, is a difficult component of the job, but having to deal with a client who is clearly grieving during and following euthanasia and other traumatic events can be draining on veterinary staff. Contributing further to this is cases where the owner would like to remain with their deceased pet for some time after the euthanasia, but the vet requires the room to treat other patients. Being able to balance the right amount of respect and assertiveness can be crucial at times like these.

### Work demands

Working long hours, working at a fast pace, the complexity of work, and the volume of work are frequently reported by vets as significant issues. Working as a vet can involve significant work demands — particularly when you consider dealing with owners and clients, and the unrealistic expectations that can be placed on the vet. The nature of specialisation and the location of a vet's practice can also have an impact. Most vets report finding their jobs very demanding. Recent research has found that working long hours may be directly linked to the psychological health of vets and their levels of depression, anxiety, and overall mental health.

Work demands include the general workload of consulting with clients back-to-back, dealing with unexpected emergencies, as well as having to return phone calls, perform follow-up calls, arrange referrals, deal with staff and other issues, and running a practice. Vets sometimes also work within organisations that are poorly managed, with many veterinary practices being small businesses with the owners or managers having little skills in management — and little understanding of people's needs within a team of vets.

One improvement in overall work demand has been the advent of after-hours emergency centres, which have reduced the requirement for many vets to be on-call and work long into the night. Unfortunately, however, the nature of places such as animal emergency centres and pounds can mean an increased likelihood of having to perform euthanasia.

### Unrealistic expectations on one's self

Apart from dealing with unrealistic expectations from owners, there is evidence that some vets are placing unrealistic expectations on themselves, as well as having unrealistic expectations placed on them by other staff and employers. This is not limited to the medical aspects of veterinary care however, as some vets are also expected to reach a certain level of product sales on top of their already demanding work day. It should be noted that a lot of vets tend to be high achievers who tend to lean toward a self-expectance that because of their high-achieving nature, they should perform at unrealistic levels. Once they realise this is not always possible and they are not miracle workers, it can act as a self-defeating prophecy. Furthermore, some vets have reported that it can be distressing when clients expect them to make all the decisions for them, particularly when this relates to euthanasia of the owner's pet.

### Lack of personal support

Awareness of what mental health support mechanisms are in place for vets varies amongst the profession. The services available via member organisations such as the Australian Veterinary Association or the American Veterinary Medical Association vary also. It is important therefore that relevant veterinary membership and training organisations continue to reach out to working vets with information and advice on where to seek help if needed. As in the case with all examples of mental distress, a lack of appropriate support whether from friends, family, colleagues or in the form of professional therapy places a stressful burden on individual suffering.

## Lack of knowledge

A perceived lack of knowledge about one's profession is often expressed in the early stages of a professional's career, particularly just after graduation. For vets that can mean being expected to diagnose and treat animals without being certain of what it is they are treating. In my own clinical work, I have been struck by how often even experienced vets might question their ability when treating animals, wondering if they are accurately diagnosing the issue at hand.

## Work/life balance

Possibly more salient before the advent of after-hours emergency care centres and for those working in remote, rural, or isolated locations where they may be the only vet on duty, is the importance of a good work/life balance. Work/life balance does not necessarily mean 50% of the time spent at work and 50% of time spent at home. Instead, it is about being able to maintain an appropriate balance between the two that works well for you. Unfortunately, the uncertainty of what to expect each day within a veterinary practice can have an impact on this balance, as often staff are expected or required to work beyond their regular work hours to meet client demands. Other times, vets may be required to make house calls on their way home from work, which can negatively impact the time they get to spend with their own family.

## Location of practice and area of specialisation

For those working in rural, remote, or isolated locations — or in the case of a particular level of expertise being required (such as small animal vet, equine vet, and so forth), additional demands on the vet can take their toll.

## Loneliness

Even though many vets work within a practice in the presence of other staff, they may, in fact, be primarily working on their own when consulting with clients, creating a feeling of loneliness. In a busy practice with clients booked back-to-back, there is little time left to be able to talk informally and formally with colleagues in the practice.

*Family and relationship issues*

Families and relationships can be impacted by the demands required of a vet, however, as with some of the factors addressed above the advent of after-hours emergency care centres, has reduced the times that vets are required to be on after-hours call. Nevertheless, vets report that they feel their family and partners do need to have a certain level of understanding and provide a level of support, particularly when they have experienced a distressing day with their clients. Unfortunately, the unpredictable working hours that sometimes occur result in some vets not being home in time to put their children to bed, or to help prepare dinner or undertake other chores — subsequently placing undesirable pressure on both themselves and their loved ones. This is particularly concerning since staying connected to your colleagues, family, partner, and friends is recognised as having a positive effect on happiness. Such relationships also form a 'support network' to assist in avoiding emotional isolation.

*Lack of effective coping strategies*

In a crisis, most vets are aware that emergency support from others is always available via phone from such organisations in Australia as Lifeline or BeyondBlue. For everyday vet work pressure, behavioural strategies such as going home and having a quiet glass of wine or making sure to spend quality time with their loved ones are common and can have some impact. Most of the vets I have dealt with in my work, however, express an unawareness of any effective personal psychological coping strategies to deal with severe stress they may sometimes experience.

One coping strategy often overlooked though is asking for help. Vets tend to be very independent, and as such often find it difficult to ask for help or even see the benefits of asking for help. It is an issue I see in my work as a psychologist — we are used to being the problem-solvers, the helper of others, the ones who are expected to have all the answers for our clients. With this comes the perception that we 'should', 'must', or 'have to' be able to sort out our issues independently. But notice here I said 'perception' — as that is what it is — a perception which is not necessarily a reality. It is unrealistic to think we should, must, or have, to work out the problems we have on our own without seeking support from other people. The other perception is that seeking help is a sign of weakness. Yet the opposite is true. People who have the courage to speak up and admit they aren't coping on their own and need a little bit of support show that they value themselves and their wellbeing enough to stand up and keep fighting.

## Students and Recent Graduates

As noted in Chapter 1, the risks to mental health and wellbeing of vets have been shown to be present upon graduation. It is important therefore to consider the stress on those upon the cusp of entering the profession or in the first year of practice.

For vet students, managing potential conflict between human and animal interests, as well as juggling the different work-related, academic, professional, or interpersonal demands, are likely to lead to an increased level of stress. When considering those who are new vet graduates, initially there may be a lot of enthusiasm, but research has shown there is a gradual loss of commitment, energy, and idealism over time, which tends to shorten veterinary careers. It has been suggested that the curriculums of veterinary schools should be modified to incorporate the teaching of individual coping and cognitive skills to undergraduates, with the possibility and opportunity to enhance such skills during their later career. Such an approach will also be able to give young vets the capacity to cope with changes within the workplace in an effort to increase work satisfaction, job engagement, and improved mental health.

## Major Strengths Supporting Vet Wellbeing

Having looked at the stressful issues facing the veterinary profession, it is also important to note that vets who manage that unique stress better than others exhibit certain traits, qualities, skills and attributes that can be identified. These also help point us in the right direction when considering how best to tackle the 'dark side.'

Research from veterinary schools has identified a 'top 10' of qualities associated with a vet who is described as 'thriving'.

- **Business acumen.** Possessing sharp business skills and managing the demands of a veterinary clinic.

- **Communication skills.** Having excellent communication skills to enable vets to talk effectively with clients about a range of issues.

- **Compassion.** Being compassionate and putting owners and animals at ease.

- **Customer service skills.** Being able to satisfy the client's animal care needs.

- **Dedication.** Having a sense of dedication to the profession.

- **Good manual dexterity.** Ability to restrain animals of all sizes and performing procedures with ease.

- **Passion for animals.** Being passionate about animals and having a commitment to provide the best care for them.

- **Quick decision-making skills.** Responding and making decisions efficiently and effectively.

- **Thorough knowledge.** Possessing a thorough knowledge of behaviours, anatomy, and ailments of different animals.

- **Time-management skills.** Balancing the demands of a busy appointment schedule. The type of person who becomes a vet is likely to have consideration for the owners of animals and be genuinely committed to animal wellbeing. The ability to effectively manage their time is therefore crucial.

We can also define some specific skills and attributes valued by the profession by looking at the requirements for entry into pursuing postgraduate studies in veterinary medicine, such as for the Doctor of Veterinary Medicine (DVM) degrees which require:

- having a high level of compassion for both animals and people,

- having high levels of ethical and moral standards,

- possessing excellent communication and interpersonal skills,

- expecting to effectively interact with people of all religious, cultural, ethnic, and social backgrounds, and

- a motivation to serve.

At one veterinary college (Cornell College of Veterinary Medicine), it is highlighted that vet students must also be able to demonstrate skills and abilities in communication, motor, observation, social and behaviour, and intellectual activities.

This emphasis on personal qualities, as opposed to knowledge of anatomy and disease for example, is also reflected in reports that employers of new vet graduates value interpersonal and personal attributes over academic capabilities. Teamwork, self-confidence, interpersonal skills, reliability, punctuality, initiative, and cheerful personality are all deemed to be highly desirable by employers in the veterinary profession. Unfortunately, research has also shown that some new graduates express a mismatch between the reality of veterinary practice and their expectations — with most recent graduates generally reporting their work was more money oriented, stressful, and emotional than expected.

This financial focus is seen within the following list of 'successful character traits for vets' compiled a few years ago by vet and practice consultant Keith Webb.

- **Sales focused.** Vets who are successful understand that 99% of failure or success in any type of vet practice is related to their ability to successfully sell their service or product.

- **Results oriented.** Successful vets realise there are no failures in telephone conversion or marketing — only results, which is why they monitor progress, learn from everything they do, and test new ideas continually. In addition, they understand each phone call, advertisement, and correspondence draws them closer to a winning sales formula.

- **Persistence.** Successful vets persist with marketing and telephone conversion, making a solid commitment to continue until they succeed.

- **Strong belief.** The most successful, or top, practice owners believe in themselves, their services, their clients, and their products. They also believe in changing lives for the better through the power of information.

- **Activity focused.** Successful vets tend to put their focus into sales-related activities, including correspondence and follow-up phone calls.

- **Fun and friendly.** The more fun you have, the more likely you are to have more success from increased sales — this is due to people loving to buy from those they have fun with and trust.

- **Have a purpose.** Having a purpose, a reason why, or a grand quest that motivates you daily.

- **Honesty and trust/dependability.** Earning trust helps to build trust with clients — one way to do this is to deliver on promises.

Yet this list again includes personal attributes separate to just making money. In my own experience, I have come across a perceived conflict whereby a focus on sales and marketing means less time on the treatment of animals. For example, a vet working in a large practice may feel being given an increase in KPIs (key performance indicators) places more responsibility and expectation on them — taking away their ability to be genuine, authentic, and client-centred. Yet focusing on personal traits while undertaking the business essentials of a practice can contribute positively to both financial and personal outcomes.

When you have a bit of fun and build trust with your customers, they in turn will start to trust you. I have personally found that when someone takes the time to follow up with me on something or delivers on their promises, it also helps to build my trust in them. This doesn't just apply to sales or face-to-face interactions. It also includes social media. I try and make it a point to respond to all comments left on my social media posts — after all, how frustrating is it when you see the account holder posting away all different things, to which their followers take the time to respond to, only to be ignored as if they are not important. I have found over the years that this builds trust and respect, and my followers appreciate the fact that their comments are read and responded to on most occasions.

## Professional support mechanisms

The tendency for vets to not seek out help early enough when facing mental distress as noted in Chapter 1 can be combatted in some way by continuing research to better understand the mental health and wellbeing of vets. Not only is this research revealing targets for intervention and suggestions for training, it is also causing much more to be said and written about the issue. This in turn can help reduce the stigma vets feel in relation to mental health issues mitigating the negative impact on a person's decision about whether they will reach out for support or not. Overcoming that stigma then requires adequate support mechanisms be in place for those seeking help.

Within Australia, at the time of writing this book, members of the Australian Veterinary Association can access a free, confidential telephone counselling service for support. There are also some veterinary practices who offer free counselling through their workplace wellbeing programs under an Employee Assistance Program (EAP). I have personally worked for most of the major EAP providers in Australia and find these services can be very beneficial. Additionally, one of the aims with my *Love Your Pet Love Your Vet* charity is to be able to fund psychological and educational support for veterinary professionals. I also work one-on-one with veterinary professionals to provide individualised, confidential, and non-judgemental support via my wellbeing sessions.

In the United Kingdom, there are various sources of support, such as:

- A 24-hour helpline which is staffed by trained volunteers from the veterinary profession.

- A health support program for the treatment and support of addiction and mental health-related issues.

- A benevolent fund to provide financial assistance in times of hardship to vets and their families.

- A dedicated website 'Vetlife' for support information available to veterinary professionals.

- A graduate support scheme supporting graduates up to eight years post-graduation.

In the US, the American Veterinary Medical Association (AVMA) report that a number of states have wellbeing programs available for veterinary professionals and their families, with a link provided on their website for further information (www.avma.org). Additionally, they report that through the University of Tennessee Veterinary Social Work program a veterinary social worker from the Knoxville School of Veterinary Social Work at the University of Tennessee, is accessible to any veterinarian — regardless of whether they are graduates from that university.

Such support mechanisms are a start and provide vital assistance. Yet more must be done to provide adequate, appropriate, and well-researched intervention strategies that are readily accepted and make a difference.

### Personal support mechanisms

There is little information known about what strategies vets use to cope with the stress of their profession, and interestingly, veterinary students in Australia have been found to be inconsistent in the range of coping strategies they use to handle the stressors experienced throughout their veterinary studies. However, when encountering periods of work-related stress in New Zealand, vets have been shown how to seek assistance and information, as well as make good use of their social networks. These social networks tend to be from informal sources such as family, colleagues, and friends as opposed to those from more formal sources such as counsellors, telephone helplines, and health professionals. It is thought that while professional assistance is available, vets who develop and maintain close personal relationships early in their careers are likely to have built for themselves an effective preventative and coping strategy.

Despite the evidence of challenges to their mental health and wellbeing, seeking professional help is not always the first consideration of vets when under stress. In my own research and practice, I have found that a lot of vets have high levels of pride and a mindset driven by high intelligence and high achieving personalities. This can lead them to believe they should be able to deal effectively with any problem that comes their way — without seeking the help of anyone else. Sadly, this leads to many vets suffering in silence unnecessarily, which then has a flow-on effect to their colleagues, clients, families, friends, and so on.

## The Next Step

As revealed above, vets work in high-stress environments with a multitude of factors demanding their attention and focus. They tend to be high-achievers, with many expectations placed on them from both themselves and other people. Sadly, these issues contribute to the high levels of suicide within the profession, and little has previously been done to provide adequate, appropriate, and well-researched intervention strategies that are readily accepted. In the development of my *Coping and Wellbeing Program for Veterinary Professionals* I felt it was important to note that not all vets suffer unduly. Some vets are seemingly able to cope well with their job, while others falter, some dangerously so.

The field of positive psychology provides some answers to this reality and contributes to one of the four core psychological approaches of the program. The next section covering Chapters 3, 4, 5, and 6, explores these core approaches and how they contribute practical tools to use in your everyday life and practice toward building and maintaining your mental health and wellbeing. As a brief introduction, and to leave you with a taste of what can be done to help vets, here are a few tips from positive psychology to help enhance your coping skills right now:

- **Looking after your physical health and getting enough sleep.** While diet and exercise are important, it is equally important to plan time for relaxation each day — as little as 15 minutes per day can make a difference.

- **Keeping a sense of perspective.** Does everything really matter? While experience shows the negative feelings in our lives tend to pass, it is beneficial to see these as a learning curve and be able to enjoy life again. We should aim to avoid becoming trapped in a state of perfectionism, and instead be satisfied with 'good enough'.

- **Regularly engage yourself in activities that create 'flow'.** Being in a state of flow indicates we are fully immersed in a task we find rewarding, and therefore we forget everything else going on in our lives. In doing so, we become focused on the present moment, rather than getting caught up in the past, or worrying about the future — both of which cannot be controlled.

- **Savour, be grateful for, and reflect upon the good things in life.** No matter how small they may be, it is important to be able to acknowledge things in your life for which you can be grateful. Activities such as keeping a gratitude journal, or jotting down three good things each day, can be helpful.

- **Do not expect money to bring you happiness.** Unfortunately, material wealth fails to produce long-lasting happiness, and we can become habituated with continual envy of those who are better off than ourselves.

- **Engage in meaningful activities.** Meaningful activities are those you find challenging, offer security, are motivating, and which you can undertake with some autonomy and a feeling of pride.

- **Be yourself and be content with who you are.** You will forever feel like someone else's prisoner if all you care about is getting the approval of other people. Instead, focus on your personal strengths and talents, and live your life in a way that enables you to fully utilise them.

- **Develop a sense of control.** Having a sense of control has been linked to both psychological and physical health. Therefore, it is important to realise that you do have some influence over what happens to you.

- **Learn to be optimistic.** You can learn to become more optimistic, but I believe you should also remain realistic while being positive. If you struggle with optimism, there are resources available which can help, such as Martin Seligman's book *Learned Optimism*.

- **Give yourself regular treats.** I believe it is important to reward yourself. However you should not become stuck in the sole pursuit of pleasure by only doing those things that bring immediate feelings of pleasure and gratification.

- **Simplify.** Learn how to say 'no' without feeling guilty and try not to squeeze more and more activities into less and less time. Developing effective time-management strategies could help with this, and which I will cover in Section 4 of this book.

- **Only take time to choose carefully when the decision is important.** If the decision you need to make is relatively inconsequential, try to settle for 'good enough', rather than making sure your choice is 'perfect' (after all, is there any such thing as perfect anyway?).

- **Be good to others.** A key ingredient of happiness is being kind and of service to other people regularly. One suggestion you can try is a random act of kindness, which is said to enhance your level of wellbeing. Your act of kindness does not have to include something of a monetary nature (although it can, such as paying for someone else's coffee), but could also be a kind gesture like letting someone be served before you at the checkout or helping a colleague at work if you can.

# SECTION THREE


# What Can help

# Chapter 3

# Positive Psychology

In 1998, Martin Seligman formerly introduced positive psychology as a major theme while serving as president of the American Psychological Association. Along with fellow psychologists Mihaly Csikszentmihalyi, Christopher Petersen, Barabara Fredickson and others, Seligman's championing of an alternative to a focus on mental illness has developed into 'the scientific study of optimal human functioning that aims to discover the factors that allow individuals and communities to thrive'. At the subjective level, positive psychology is about wellbeing, satisfaction, and contentment (in the past), flow and happiness (in the present), and hope and optimism (for the future). At the group level, positive psychology is about civic virtues, and at the individual level, it is about positive individual traits. Additionally, positive psychology is about happiness, with wellbeing and happiness the desired outcomes. Seligman describes three desirable lives, which he calls the 'pleasant life', the 'good life', and the 'meaningful life'. Wellbeing and happiness are used interchangeably in relation to the pleasant life and are overarching terms in describing the entire goals of positive psychology.

The scientific discipline of applied positive psychology focuses on an improvement in functioning, rather than the more traditional clinical psychological focuses on the disease model. In this way it is not just the study of weakness, damage, and pathology, but also the study of virtue and strength. Treatment is not just about fixing what is wrong, but also about nurturing what is best. It is also about education, work, love, insight, growth, and play. The pleasurable, positive experiences in life should be distinguished from enjoyable, positive experiences. It is enjoyment, rather than pleasure, that leads to personal growth and long-term happiness. The intention of positive psychology then is to have a more balanced and complete scientific understanding of the peaks, valleys, and in-betweens of the human experience — something most vets can certainly relate to.

There is now persuasive evidence that psychological and physical health can be protected by factors such as believing in a sense of personal control and optimism. More recently, it has emerged that happiness is causal and can bring many more benefits to people than just feeling good. Happy people are found to be more successful, healthier, and socially engaged. Positive psychology divides happiness into three different realms, described as hedonic (which are positive emotions such as joy, contentment, pleasure, and love), the state of flow — that is, about being engaged with an activity and losing self-consciousness throughout, and the meaningful life — feeling like you have a sense of belonging and are serving something you believe is bigger than yourself.

Positive psychology also adopts the use of character strengths and virtues (CSV), and envisages that the CSV will 'do for psychological well-being what the DSM of the American Psychological Association does for psychological disorders that disable human beings'. The CSV classifies and describes virtues and strengths that enable humans to thrive, and refers to six overarching virtues that virtually every human culture worldwide endorses: wisdom, humanity, courage, justice, transcendence, and temperance. Under each of these virtues are 24 character strengths, which will be discussed later.

There have however been criticisms of positive psychology, with some suggesting that if there is such thing as 'positive' psychology, then all other psychology must be 'negative' psychology, and that those who study positive psychology prefer a 'Pollyanna' view of the world and fail to recognise the negative aspects of life. It has also been suggested that goal achievement, goal setting, and motivation are concepts of dubious explanatory value and that problems arise when accounts of happiness (determined by way of an optimistic and positive attitude) are used to describe mental health which can be achieved by 're-crafting' one's attitude.

We are all of course free to make up our minds and have our own opinions on the topic of positive psychology, however as well as a growing body of quality research, many practising psychologists including myself have directly experienced and witnessed the benefits of using positive psychology interventions. In the rest of this chapter I will outline the essential elements that make up the concept of positive psychology to illustrate how its application to the enhancement of wellbeing in vets is appropriate. Positive psychology offers a range of effective strategies and a focus on what is essentially right in your life, helping to prevent you getting caught up with what is not going so well.

## Authentic Happiness Theory to Wellbeing Theory

In his 2011 book *Flourish*, Seligman further refined the concept of positive psychology and concluded that happiness alone does not give us meaning, although it is still part of wellbeing. He has since renamed his earlier 'authentic happiness theory', 'wellbeing theory', explaining that there were three inadequacies in authentic happiness theory.

Firstly, the popular connotation of happiness (which had been the dominant focus of the area) is ultimately tied up with being in a cheerful mood. At the bottom of happiness is positive emotion. Critics have reported that authentic happiness theory redefines happiness by including the desiderata of meaning and engagement to supplement positive emotion. It is suggested that while neither meaning or engagement refers to how one feels, and while they may be desirable, they are not — nor can they ever be — part of what is denoted by happiness.

Secondly, life satisfaction is held in too-privileged a place when measuring happiness. In authentic happiness theory, happiness is operationalised as the gold standard of life satisfaction, which is measured by a widely researched self-report scale. The overarching goal of positive psychology follows on from that gold standard, which is to increase life satisfaction universally. However, as Seligman reports, the level of life satisfaction people feel is instead determined by how good they felt when they were asked that question. Therefore, when averaged over a range of people, it was found that 70 per cent of how much life satisfaction is reported is determined by the mood the respondent is in, and 30 per cent is how well that person will judge their life at that particular moment. Hence the original gold standard view of positive psychology was tied disproportionately to mood.

Thirdly, positive emotion, engagement, and meaning do not deplete those things that individuals choose merely for their own sake.

Authentic happiness theory was thus an attempt to explain happiness, with life satisfaction being its defining feature. Those who have the most meaning, the most positive emotion, and the most engagement, also had the most life satisfaction and were deemed the happiest. In contrast, wellbeing theory instead asserts that wellbeing is a construct which has several measurable elements, each making a contribution — but none of which define wellbeing in themselves. Therefore, it is not the entity of life satisfaction that is the focus of positive psychology, but the construct of wellbeing.

## PERMA

According to Seligman, there are several major contributing factors to wellbeing. In being able to flourish, wellbeing takes centre stage, and with that, five pillars of positive psychology (termed PERMA) become the permanent building blocks for a fulfilled life. Each of these five pillars of wellbeing contains three properties. These pillars are Positive Emotion, Engagement, Meaning, Positive Relationships, and Accomplishment.

### Positive Emotion

Positive emotion essentially represents the *pleasant life*. This element was included in the original authentic happiness theory and remains a cornerstone of wellbeing theory. Encompassed in positive emotion are the normal subjective wellbeing variables such as comfort, joy, serenity, ecstasy, warmth, pleasure, and so on.

### Engagement

Undertaking activities we enjoy and that require our full engagement is seen as essential to personal happiness. Unlike using the present moment for pleasure states, engagement is viewed retrospectively, but subjectively.

### Positive Relationships

This element is ultimately about other people. When thinking about positive things, very little of these are solitary. For example, when you think about laughing uncontrollably, or experience immense joy, meaning, or purpose, or feel incredibly proud of something you have achieved, these events all take place around others. Similarly, the best antidote to life's downers and reliable uppers are other people.

### Meaning

Meaning could be included as a positive emotion due to its subjective component. However is not only a subjective state, as a subjective judgement can be contradicted by a more objective and dispassionate judgement of coherence, history, and logic. This element is about our meaning and purpose in life — what are you here for, what do you want to stand for?

### Accomplishment

Accomplishment is often sought just for the sake of achieving something, even if it does not bring meaning, positive emotion, or anything in the way of positive relationships. However, to flourish in life, we need to seek to achieve in life the things that give us a sense of satisfaction.

## Positive Education

With respect to education, positive psychology says that wellbeing is synergistic with improved learning. If wellbeing is increased, the likely outcome is an increase in learning. It is believed that a positive mood results in broader attention and improves creative and holistic thinking. This is in contrast to negative moods, which are said to produce narrower attention, and more analytical and critical thinking. Think about your thoughts when you are feeling positive versus negative — can you relate? Also think about how your mood affected or affects (if you are still a student) your education — do you notice any correlation?

Furthermore, it is proposed that wellbeing can be taught, and should be taught — firstly as an antidote to depression, secondly as a vehicle for increasing satisfaction in life, and thirdly as an aid to more creative thinking and better learning. There is indeed also a growing scientific basis for understanding meaning, positive emotion, and engagement, which are each valuable in their own right as they assist with promoting learning, fighting depression, and engendering more life satisfaction. As an example of this, the Penn Resiliency Program was created to promote optimism by teaching students how to be flexible and think more realistically about their problems. The program also teaches students how to make decisions, brainstorm creatively, be assertive, and adopt several other problem-solving and coping skills. The major goals of the program are to assist students in identifying their character strengths and increase the use of these strengths in students' day-to-day lives to promote positive emotion, resilience, and a sense of purpose or meaning.

Hope and optimism have been reported as gaining attention as important variables in positive psychology, as they are variables that can be malleable to the influence of teachers, as well as having an effect on academic achievement. Within Australia and overseas schools have implemented a range of resiliency programs influenced by positive psychology such as the Penn Resiliency Program. New programs for schools continue to be developed.

It is no surprise then that introducing education strategies from positive psychology into tertiary level veterinary training should be a priority in the fight against the negative impacts on wellbeing explored earlier in this book.

## The Core Virtues of Positive Psychology

Positive psychology defines six core virtues, and 24 character strengths, which have revealed an amount of similarity across cultures, strongly indicating a cross-cultural and historical convergence. The six core virtues and respective character strengths are summarised in Table 3.1.

### Courage

There are said to be three types of courage — moral, psychological, and physical. *Moral* courage involves being able to maintain ethical authenticity or integrity while at the risk of losing employment, prestige, privacy, or

**Table 3.1   The Core Virtues of Positive Psychology**

| Virtue | Character Strengths |
| --- | --- |
| Courage | Bravery (valour), persistence (perseverance, industriousness), integrity (authenticity, honesty), vitality (zest, enthusiasm, vigour, energy) |
| Justice | Citizenship (social responsibility, loyalty, teamwork), fairness, leadership |
| Humanity | Love, kindness (generosity, nurturance, care, compassion, altruistic love, niceness), social intelligence (emotional intelligence, personal intelligence) |
| Temperance | Forgiveness and mercy, humility/modesty, prudence, self-regulation (self-control) |
| Transcendence | Appreciation of beauty and excellence (awe, wonder, elevation), gratitude, hope (optimism, future-mindedness, future orientation), humour (playfulness), spirituality (religiousness, faith, purpose) |
| Wisdom and Knowledge | Creativity (originality, ingenuity), curiosity (interest, novelty-seeking, openness to experience), open-mindedness (judgement, critical thinking), love of learning, perspective (wisdom) |

friends. *Psychological* courage is defined as that required to be able to confront a destructive situation or habit or illness and being brave in the face of one's inner demons. *Physical* courage involves overcoming the fear of death or physical injury in pursuit of saving oneself or another person.

Courage is not only seen externally but also has an inner life. This is to say that it is not just the observable acts that comprise courage, but also the decisions, emotions, motivations, and cognitions that bring them about. The following character strengths are incorporated under this core virtue.

*Bravery (valour)*

Typically and historically, bravery is viewed as the physical valour displayed by warriors doing battle on the battlefield. The bravery displayed when faced with imminent death is not the equivalent of fearlessness, as the person in this situation may certainly experience fear. Viewing bravery in this way allows the strength to be used beyond the domain of battle to doing or saying the correct, but unpopular thing, resisting peer pressure when it comes to a morally questionable shortcut, and facing a terminal illness with composure. The strength of bravery has also been described as the disposition to act voluntarily, and potentially fearfully, in dangerous situations when risks are reasonably appraised, while endeavouring to preserve or obtain something which is perceived to be good for others or oneself, and understanding that this perceived good may not be realised. Its essence is that it speaks across cultures, disciplinary divides, and social and work settings.

### Persistence (industriousness, perseverance)

This character strength involves taking care of business, keeping-on despite any obstacles, finishing what has been started, staying on track, and finishing what has been started. It is defined as the continuation of action that is voluntary and goal-directed, despite discouragement, obstacles, and difficulties. Perseverance and persistence are used interchangeably in this regard, although perseverance is regarded a little more narrowly. Perseverance can be described as a continually repeated action that is essentially a default response.

### Integrity (honesty, authenticity)

This character strength is regarded more broadly than someone who speaks the truth and is honest. It does involve being truthful but also involves taking responsibility for what one does, and how one feels. It includes presenting oneself genuinely to others, and the sense of being a morally coherent individual. Authenticity, honesty, and integrity all capture a character trait where individuals are true to themselves, and represent their intentions, commitments, and internal states accurately — both publicly and privately. These people take ownership and responsibility for their own behaviours and feelings, and by doing so, reap substantial benefits.

### Vitality (vigour, energy, zest, enthusiasm)

This is a different sort of strength as it is just as much a part of the mind as it is the body. Vitality is regarded as being full of zest, displaying enthusiasm for all and any activities, and feeling alive — it is a dynamic aspect of well-being which is indicated subjectively by the experience of aliveness and energy. People with this character strength are normally described as energetic and vigorous, bouncy and perky, high on life, peppy, and bright-eyed and bushy-tailed. It must be noted, however, that vitality in this context is different from nervous energy, tension, mania, or hyperactivity. It is described as enthusiasm *about*, and zest *for*.

## Justice

This core virtue generally refers to those things that make life fair. While we are aware that life is not always fair, we need a more pragmatic approach where the laws provide a fair shot for everyone. Justice exemplars are civic in nature, such as leadership, citizenship, fairness, and teamwork. The following character strengths are incorporated under this core virtue.

### Citizenship (loyalty, social responsibility, teamwork)

The strength of citizenship incorporates a sense of, and identification with, the obligation to a common good that stretches beyond an individual's personal membership interests, where they are a member of their family, with colleagues, fellow tenants in apartment buildings, others that share the same ethnic heritage, possibly the entire human race, and themselves. Individuals that possess this character strength contribute equally to others in a group and have a strong sense of duty because they believe this is what should be done as a group member. Rather than working for personal gain, individuals with this strength work for the good of the group.

### Fairness

Fairness relates to a person's treatment of others in identical or similar ways. For example, not letting your issues or personal feelings bias your decisions. A product of moral judgement, fairness is the process by which individuals ascertain what is morally right and wrong, as well as what is prescribed morally. Desirable developmental outcomes of a person's commitment to fairness in their social relations is the ability to come to embody caring and compassion for others, being sensitised to issues of social injustice, and having the perceptiveness required for relational understanding.

### Leadership

As individuals, we belong to numerous social groups, many of which are structured hierarchically with an informal or formal leader who directs and dictates the activities of its followers. There are two tasks of any leader that have been distinguished by leadership theorists, which are: preserving and creating good relationships and morale amongst its members and having the members of the group do what they should be doing. As a personal quality, leadership refers to an integrated constellation of temperament and cognitive attributes which adopt an orientation toward motivating and directing others' actions toward collective success, as well as influencing and helping others. People with the strength of leadership can comfortably manage their own activities, as well as those of others.

## Humanity

Humanity and justice are separated, despite both involving the improvement of another's welfare. In this respect, humanity is referred to as the virtues involved in how we relate to others — that is, interpersonal strengths. Within psychology, virtues of humanity are rendered as prosocial or altruistic behaviour, and there are many species (not just primates) whose behaviour appears to reflect altruism. These strengths also include the positive traits which are manifested when someone is in a caring relationship with others. The following character strengths are incorporated under this core virtue.

### Love

This strength, in its most developed form, happens when there is a reciprocal relationship with another person. It excludes crushes, stalking, worship, unrequited love, hero worship, and being a fan of someone, as these feelings are only one-sided. Rather, this strength incorporates romantic friendship and love, mentoring relationships, the love between children and parents, and emotional connections between co-workers and teammates. Three prototypical forms of love can be seen — one is the love we have for those who are our primary source of care, affection, and protection — those who make us feel safe, such as a child's love for a parent. Another type of love is for those who are dependent on us to make them feel cared for and safe, such as a parent's love for a child. The third form of love is romantic love, which is the type that involves passionate desires for emotional, physical, and sexual closeness with someone who makes us feel special, and someone we consider to be special.

### Kindness (compassion, care, nurturance, generosity, altruistic love, niceness)

This strength is described as the inclination to be compassionate and concerned about other people's welfare, being nice, performing good deeds, taking care of, and doing favours for, other people. It can include a brief encounter directed towards a stranger, such as giving up our seat for someone else, or the establishment of a significant gift, such as donating a kidney to a close friend or relative. The terms used in this character strength are networked closely and related to terms that indicate a common orientation of the self toward someone else. Kindness and altruistic love both require the affirmation that there is a common humanity where others are worthy of affirmation and attention for no other reason but their own sake.

### Social intelligence (personal intelligence, emotional intelligence)

Individuals who are in emotional intelligence display special capacities in relation to strategising and experiencing emotion. They can perceive emotions in relationships, and display a good understanding of the emotional relationships they have with others, together with what the meanings within these relationships equate to emotionally. Intelligence is referred to as being able to think in an abstract manner — that is, being able to understand the differences and similarities between things, seeing other relations, and being able to recognise these patterns.

## Temperance

This virtue is the control over excess, commonly described as: 'everything in moderation'. While it is used to signify abstinence, especially from activities such as smoking, sex, drinking, and eating, in this regard it is termed more generally to incorporate any aspect of auspicious self-restraint. As an example, within psychological terminology, temperance becomes translated into self-regulation or self-efficacy, which is the ability to manage and monitor one's emotions, behaviour, and motivation without the input of outside assistance. Failure to do so can lead to all kinds of social and personal problems. The following character strengths are incorporated under this core virtue.

### Forgiveness and mercy

An individual who has never been wronged by anyone else is very fortunate, and because there has been no offence, there is no need to forgive. Likewise, the person who has never been able to exact revenge on others who have done wrong is also fortunate. There is no need to be merciful because no punishment can suspend, cancel, or minimise. However, most people find themselves in situations where forgiveness and mercy is or is not enacted. Those who display forgiveness and mercy are those who consistently let things be — not out of fear, guilt, permissiveness, or shame, nor out of external incentives such as bribes, threats, or being awarded damages in civil suits — but rather from a positive strength of character.

### Humility and modesty

This character strength is referred to as a quiet strength, as people who are modest do not seek the limelight, and they are able to let their accomplishments speak for themselves. They can acknowledge any imperfections and mistakes, and regard themselves as being fortunate enough that something good has happened to them, rather than taking undue credit for their accomplishments. To be modest and humble does not relate to self-humiliation or self-derogation, but instead leads to a presentation of oneself in an important, but accurate, way that deflects the attention from themselves and onto other circumstances or people. A person who is humble or modest is generally authentic and honest, but an authentic and honest person is not necessarily modest and humble.

### Prudence

Occasionally prudence has a bad reputation, such as when labelling a person a prude is not really praising them! Prudes are labelled as uptight, overly cautious, timid, and boring. As a character strength though, the prudent person keeps in mind what will eventually develop the most satisfaction, and they will not sacrifice long-term goals for short-term pleasures. They make smart choices rather than no choices at all. It is a personal cognitive orientation to the future, in a type of self-management and practical reasoning which helps the individual to effectively achieve their long-term goals. The person who is prudent shows deliberate and far-sighted concern for the consequences of their decisions and actions, and can resist other choices and impulses which successfully satisfies short-term goals at the expense of their long-term goals. The can also demonstrate a moderate and flexible approach to life.

### Self-regulation (self-control)

The person who exercises self-regulation exerts control over their own responses to enable them to pursue goals and live up to certain standards. Such responses include those which could be occasioned by extreme emotions and impulses. Sometimes self-control is referred to as a synonym for self-regulation, and other times it is used more finely to specifically refer to behaving in a moral fashion and controlling one's impulses. The responses included in self-regulation can include emotions, performances, thoughts, impulses, and other behaviours. The standards incorporate moral injunctions, performance targets, norms, ideals, and other people's expectations.

## Transcendence

The virtue of transcendence is defined broadly as the belief there is a purpose or meaning larger than ourselves, or a connection to something higher than ourselves. It is the opposite of nihilism — the contention that life has no meaning. The following character strengths are incorporated under this core virtue.

### *Appreciation of beauty (wonder, awe, elevation)*

A person with the character strength of awe is identified as being one who appreciates and notices beauty and excellence in many aspects of life. It connects to something larger than oneself — be it performances from skilled athletes, beautiful music or art, the splendour of nature, or simply the moral brilliance of others. The individual with this character strength can find, recognise, and take pleasure in the goodness that exists in both the social and physical worlds. This strength is not to be confined to the pursuits of those with wealth — rather, the defining features of this strength are the emotional experience of wonder or awe, within the presence of excellence or beauty.

### *Gratitude*

This character strength can be described as the sense of thankfulness and joy one experiences in response to a gift they receive. The gift does not necessarily have to be something tangible, such as a present from a child on your birthday. It can also include things such as listening to the ocean on a beautiful summer day. What distinguishes gratitude is the psychological response to the gift, regardless of the nature of the gift, and the experience of the transcendent emotion of grace — that is, the sense that because of another person, we have received some benefit. In addition, there are distinctions to be made between transpersonal and personal gratitude. Transpersonal gratitude is gratefulness to a higher power, the cosmos, or God, whereas personal gratitude is where thankfulness is directed toward another person for a specific benefit they have received, or for them just being themselves.

*Hope (optimism, future orientation, future-mindedness)*

Hope and optimism are representative of an emotional, cognitive, and motivational future and the goodness it may hold. When thinking about the future, the hopeful or optimistic individual expects their desired outcomes and events will happen, they act in a manner which they believe will make their desires more likely to occur, and they feel confident that these may well ensue given their appropriate efforts to engage in good cheer in the present moment.

*Humour (playfulness)*

The character strength of humour is universal, and the humorous individual is defined as someone who is skilled at bringing a smile to the faces of other people, teasing others gently, and laughing, making jokes, and seeing the lighter side of life. This strength is said to be easier to recognise than define. It includes aspects such as being able to make others laugh or smile, playfully recognising, enjoying, and/or creating incongruity, and maintaining a cheerful and composed view of adversity that permits a person to see the lighter side of things — therefore maintaining a good mood.

*Spirituality (faith, purpose, religiousness)*

Spirituality is said to be the most human, and sublime, of all character strengths. It is defined as having coherent beliefs about the meaning of one's place within the universe and the meaning and purpose of the universe itself. It is grounded in the conviction there is a transcendent, or non-physical, dimension to life. When an individual possesses this character strength, they theorise about the meaning of life in a way that provides them comfort and shapes their conduct. Their beliefs about religiousness and spirituality are stable, persuasive, and pervasive. Spirituality is also referred to as the psychological significance and experience of ultimate beliefs.

## Wisdom and Knowledge

Wisdom can be defined as the exceptional depth and breadth of knowledge about factors of human affairs and the conditions of life, and the subsequent judgement about applying this knowledge. It can also be described as good advice and judgement about uncertain, but important, matters of life. In Peterson and Seligman's book *Character Strengths and Virtues,* they define wisdom as knowledge that is hard fought for and then used for good, and that it is a noble form of intelligence where everyone is appreciative when in its presence. The following character strengths are incorporated under this core virtue.

### Creativity (ingenuity, originality)

There are two essential components of creativity — firstly, a person who is creative produces behaviours or ideas that can be recognised as unusual, novel, or surprising. These ideas or behaviours must also be adaptable, and their originality must contribute to the individual's, or another's, life in a positive manner. It is to be noted however that originality on its own does not signify a person has creative ability. For example, individuals who suffer from severe mental disorders (such as personality disorders) can display behaviours and express ideas that can seem to be very original. This is why the second criteria of adaptability is a crucial component of this character strength. For those individuals suffering personality disorders and the like, their delusions and hallucinations lack this feature. They simply make life more problematic for the individual, rather than solving life's problems.

### Curiosity (openness to experience, novelty seeking, interest)

Curiosity can be defined as an individual's intrinsic interest in ongoing experience. Challenge, experiential novelty, and variety are all pursued by curious people. While all individuals experience curiosity, they do differ in their threshold and willingness to experience it, as well as the depth and breadth of their experience. Interest and curiosity are occasionally used interchangeably. Novelty seeking can reflect a person's tendency for pursuing exciting and novel experiences in which they elevate stimulation to optimal levels, which can include high levels of risk to benefit from acts of novelty. Openness to experience is defined as a higher order dimension of personality which incorporates a receptiveness to novel feelings, values, ideas, and fantasies.

### Open-mindedness (critical thinking, judgement)

This character strength can be described as the way an open-minded person works at the style of thinking which actively searches for evidence against their normal plans, goals, or beliefs, and when available, weighs that evidence fairly. The open-minded person is not wishy-washy, nihilistic, per-missive, or indecisive, nor do they bring this style to bear on all issues. The individual who is open-minded engages this style when they are faced with a complex judgement where the evidence for and against a particular belief needs to be weighed and examined.

### Love of learning

One way of describing this strength is that it is inherent in all human nature, particularly in the very young, to be motivated to learn about the world we have come into. However, it can also be seen across the life span as we drive forward to competently interact with the world. It is a strength that therapists encourage in their clients, that parents want to inspire in their children, that teachers would love to see their students possess, and which employers endeavour to adopt in their staff. Another view sees this character strength as a contextualised individual difference, which can be seen in certain subject matters. Individuals who possess the trait of a love of learning generally tend to be positively motivated to build on existing knowledge and skills or acquire new knowledge and skills.

### Perspective (wisdom)

While this strength is generally described by psychologists as wisdom, in this context it has been called perspective. Perspective refers to the ability to look at life and take stock in large terms that make sense to the individual and others. It is the product of experience and knowledge, but it is more than just accumulating information. That is, it is the deliberate use of the coordination of this information to improve wellbeing. Socially, it enables a person to hear what others have to say, to make an evaluation of what they have said, and then offer good advice.

## Another Step to Go

In looking at these core virtues and the character strengths postulated to support them, positive psychology provides us with a refreshing and very humanistic look at ourselves and what we do in our lives in the pursuit of happiness. But it is more than descriptive. Stemming from the applied aspects that run through all schools of clinical psychology, it offers effective strategies for building and maintaining wellbeing. Homework exercises used in positive psychology counselling and therapy may include for example writing a gratitude letter, planning your perfect day, identifying signature strengths, writing your own legacy, completing your happiness profile, writing a letter of forgiveness, changing a habit, giving the gift of time, letting go of grudges, letting others shine, and making a daily list of three good things.

While these strategies can be helpful for wellbeing and maintaining a positive and healthy mindset, I believe it is imperative that individuals have a broader skill set of strategies they can draw upon whenever the need arises. In particular, being able to address unhelpful thoughts, feelings, and behaviours is essential in everyday life. This is where *acceptance and commitment therapy* (ACT) as an intervention can play a major role alongside positive psychology. Let's take a look at what this is about in the next chapter.

# Chapter 4

# Acceptance and Commitment Therapy

cceptance and commitment therapy (ACT) is a psychological intervention developed around 30 years ago by Steven C. Hayes and colleagues. It is designed to help people move forward in a way that is
in line with their values. It helps people to become aware of their automatic
reactions by assisting them to think and feel what they are physically
thinking and feeling in that moment, rather than their assumption of what
they are thinking and feeling. Fundamentally, the acronym of ACT can be
described as:

A = Accept your feelings and thoughts and be in the present moment.

C = Choose a direction you value to move yourself forward.

T = Take action toward that valued direction.

ACT (typically pronounced as the word 'act' rather than 'A-C-T') is associated with *relational frame theory* (RFT), which is a behaviour-analytic

approach oriented to our cognitions (thoughts) and language. It refers to our specific types of relational responding as *relational frames.* When there is a consequence to an action which then results in that action increasing, this is assumed to be due to the principle of reinforcement. RFT suggests that unpleasant personal experiences such as negative thoughts or emotions can therefore be exacerbated by their learnt way of responding (that is — through reinforcement).

ACT and RFT place emphasis on the nature of human cognition and language and apply this to being able to understand and alleviate suffering. Similar to another psychological approach — *cognitive behavioural therapy* (known as CBT) — ACT focuses on emotions, behaviours, and cognitions — especially the cognitions that are closely related to causative emotional and behavioural distress. However, while it is a behavioural approach, ACT works through processes differently than other treatment interventions such as CBT.

ACT is about values-guided, and mindful, action where we can accept our internal experiences and avoidance, put our problematic and trouble-some thoughts into context, explore the goals and values we have, and commit to moving forward in the direction of our life values. Essentially, ACT aims to create a full, meaningful, and rich life while being able to accept the inevitable pain that often goes along with it.

In summary, ACT can be defined as a psychological intervention based on the concepts of modern behavioural psychology which includes RFT, and which applies methods of mindfulness and acceptance, and commit-ment and behaviour change processes — resulting in the creation of *psychological flexibility.*

## Psychological Flexibility

So what is this most important concept that ACT seeks to create and increase through therapy? Psychological flexibility enables us to have full awareness and openness to our experiences in the present moment and be able to be guided by our values to take appropriate action. In simple terms, it is defined as the ability to be present, open up, and do what matters. The more we can be open to our experience, act upon our values, and be fully conscious, the better our quality of life becomes as we are more able to respond to the challenges and problems life brings. When we are fully engaged in our life and permitting our values to guide us, we experience a sense of vitality and develop a sense of purpose and meaning. We have a sense of being fully alive, regardless of how we may be feeling in the present moment, and we can embrace the here and now.

## Mindfulness

A key focus of ACT is the mental state known as *mindfulness* which can be described as paying attention with curiosity, flexibility, and openness. Russ Harris, author of the best-selling ACT book *The Happiness Trap*, says this definition of mindfulness explains three important factors. Firstly, mindfulness is not a *thinking* process; rather it is an *awareness* process. This involves paying attention or bringing awareness to the experience you are having in the present moment, rather than being caught up in, or 'buying into' your thoughts. Secondly, an attitude of curiosity and openness is involved with mindfulness. That is, being able to be open to your experiences in the present moment, even if these are unpleasant, painful, or uncomfortable, rather than fighting with them or running away or avoiding them. Thirdly, mindfulness also involves flexibility of attention — that is, being able to broaden, direct, or focus your attention consciously on different aspects of the experience you are having.

In addition to the importance of mindfulness, there are six core processes that ACT targets in therapy with the overall objective of increasing one's psychological flexibility. In this context, psychological flexibility is the ability to contact the present moment more fully and to persist or change behaviour when it serves our values to do so. All six processes are interrelated and overlapping. Holistically, each process supports the other, and all of them are targeting psychological flexibility. It can be helpful to think of them as six facets of one diamond, and psychological flexibility is the diamond itself. Let's take a look at these core processes.

### Acceptance (the 'open up' stage)

Acceptance in ACT is taught as a substitute for experiential avoidance. It involves actively and mindfully taking on board the private events that have come about in your life, without unnecessarily trying to change their form or frequency — particularly when psychological harm would result from doing so. Acceptance means we can open up and make room for painful sensations, urges, feelings, and emotions. It allows us to stop struggling with them, give them room to breathe, and simply allow them to be just as they are. We open up to them and let them be, instead of resisting them, getting overwhelmed by them, running from them, or fighting with them. It is important to note that this process, however, does not mean we have to like or want them, rather it is to simply allow us to make room for them.

## Cognitive defusion (the 'watch your thinking' stage)

The concept of cognitive defusion (often shortened to just 'defusion') means being able to step back and detach or separate yourself from images, memories, and thoughts. Rather than buying into, or being pushed around by our thoughts, we learn to be able to let them come and go as if they were vehicles driving past our front door. We take a step back and observe our thinking as opposed to getting tangled up in it. This process also allows us to see our thoughts for what they really are — simply words or pictures. Rather than tightly clinging to them, we can loosely hold onto them instead. The techniques of cognitive defusion attempt to modify the unwelcome *aspects* of private events and thoughts, rather than attempting to modify their frequency, form, or situational sensitivity. In other words, ACT attempts to alter the way in which we relate to, or interact with, our thoughts.

## Being present (the 'be here now, contacting the present moment' phase)

The goal of being present is to enable yourself to experience your world more candidly so that your actions are more consistent with your values, and your behaviour is therefore more flexible. In this way, ACT promotes contact with environmental and psychological situations as they occur — in an ongoing and non-judgemental way. Contacting the present moment also means connecting consciously with, and engaging in, whatever is happening for you at this moment and being psychologically present. It is very difficult for humans to stay present, as we tend to get caught up in our thoughts so easily and then lose touch with what is going on around us. We may become absorbed in our thoughts about the future, or the past, and spend a lot of time doing so. Or we may just operate as if we were on automatic pilot, simply going through the motions instead of being fully conscious of our experience. When we contact the present moment, it allows us to bring flexibility to our awareness to either the psychological world within us or the physical world around us — or we may even be able to do both simultaneously. Being present means we can pay attention to our present moment, or here-and-now experiences consciously, rather than operating on automatic pilot or getting caught up in our thoughts.

### Self as context (the 'pure awareness' stage)

When we talk about the mind, we generally don't recognise the two distinct elements to it — that of the *observing self* and the *thinking self*. Most of us are aware of the thinking self, which is the part of us that is always thinking — it generates our thoughts, memories, beliefs, fantasies, plans, judgements, and so on. However, many of us are not so familiar with the observing self, which is that part of us that has an awareness of whatever we are feeling, thinking, sensing, or doing, within any given moment. As an example, as you progress and develop through life, your thoughts change, your feelings change, your body changes, and your roles change, but the part of you that never changes is the part of you that is noticing or observing all those things. It has been with you for your entire life. This concept is an important part of ACT because within this context a person can have an awareness of their own flow of experiences, but without being attached to them or having an investment in them when certain experiences occur.

### Values (the 'know what matters' stage)

Deep in your heart, do you know what you want to stand for in your life, and what you want your life to be about? What is it that you would like to do while you are on the planet for this brief time, and what really matters to you in the big picture? This is the realm of values. Values describe how you would like to act or behave on an ongoing basis, and are desired qualities of ongoing action. Being able to clarify your values is crucial in being able to develop a meaningful life. In ACT, values are often referred to as chosen life directions — they guide us on our journey through life and provide us with direction. Values are selected qualities of action that are taken purposively — they cannot be obtained as objects, rather they can be instantiated moment by moment.

### Committed action (the 'do what it takes' stage)

The final process in ACT is committed action. ACT encourages the growth of larger and larger patterns of effective action that are related to our chosen values. Committed action means taking action that is effective and guided by our values. While it is all well-and-good to know and recognise our values, our life only becomes full, meaningful, and rich via ongoing values-congruent action. Essentially, if we are only staring at the compass, we will not have much of a journey — it is only when we move our legs and arms in the direction of our choice that our journey happens. Committed action means doing what it takes — even if this brings us pain and discomfort — to live by our values. Values-guided actions also make way for a large variety of thoughts and feelings which may be pleasurable, painful, pleasant, and unpleasant. Additionally, any skill that is able to enrich and enhance life can be used in this model, such as goal setting, behavioural activation, exposure, negotiation, time management, problem-solving, assertiveness, crises coping, and self-soothing.

## Core Pathological Processes

The flip side of the six core processes that work toward enhancing psychological flexibility are six pathological processes which result from a *psychological inflexibility* of thought and behaviour. ACT theory sees the interrelated processes of *cognitive fusion* and *experiential avoidance* as being the main contributors toward psychological distress and pathology and as also giving rise to four other contributing processes.

### Fusion

The concept of fusion means we become entwined in our thoughts in a way that then dominates our awareness and has a massive influence on our behaviour. Individuals suffering from depression fuse with many kinds of unhelpful thoughts, such as 'things will never get any better' or 'everything is too hard' or 'counselling does not work'. Such individuals often become fused with painful memories, such as failure, abuse, rejection, and disappointment.

## Experiential avoidance

Experiential avoidance means trying to escape, get rid of, or avoid, unwanted private experiences such as memories, feelings, and thoughts. It is the absolute opposite of acceptance. As an example of experiential avoidance, and again using depressed people to illustrate, these individuals desperately try to get rid of or avoid painful feelings and emotions like anger, guilt, loneliness, anxiety, sadness and so on. If these feelings or emotions relate to an upcoming social event they do not wish to attend or are worried about attending, then as the social event draws closer they may become fused with unhelpful thoughts like 'I will not enjoy myself' or 'I cannot be bothered going' — the anticipation of which then results in anticipatory anxiety or dread. Therefore, they may then withdraw from the social event to avoid any feelings or thoughts they may find uncomfortable, which then provides instantaneous relief, and their unpleasant feelings and thoughts dissipate. While the relief is not long-lasting, it does provide reinforcement, thus increasing any future chance of social withdrawal. Avoidance and fusion tend to go hand in hand.

## Dominance of the conceptualised past and future/limited self-knowledge

Unfortunately, many people spend a lot of time caught up with a conceptualised past — that is, they ruminate on past events that were painful and which often involve loss, rejection, and failure (which can lead to depression). In addition, they also become fused with a conceptualised future — that is, worrying about all the terrible things that may be coming to them (which can lead to anxiety). When we are fused with our thoughts and avoid dealing with them, it can readily lead to a loss of contact with our experience in the present moment. When we dwell on events from the past that were painful and then ruminate on them (and/or start fantasising or catastrophising about the future and worrying about things that have not even happened yet), we are so focused on what we need to do next that we miss out on our life right here, right now. When we are in contact with the present moment, we include the world inside us and around us. If we lose touch with our feelings and thoughts — our inner psychological world — we lack self-knowledge. It is much more difficult to change our behaviour in adaptive ways when we lack self-knowledge.

## Lack of values clarity/contact

Our values often get forgotten, neglected, or lost when we allow our behaviour to become driven by fusing with thoughts that are unhelpful, or when we attempt to avoid private experiences that are unpleasant. We cannot use our values to effectively guide our actions if we are not in psychological contact with them, or if we are not clear about what our actual values are. For example, it is quite common for people with depression to lose touch with their values on many levels, such as being productive, taking care of their health and wellbeing, having fun, connecting with others, or engaging in activities such as hobbies, sports, and work. ACT aims to bring behaviour in line with values as opposed to avoidance or fusion. It is important to note, however, that our values should only be lightly fused with, because if we fuse with them too much they can easily become rigid rules.

## Unworkable action

Unworkable action can be described as those behavioural patterns that drag us away from valued, mindful living — that is, actions that do not work — to help our life become fuller or richer. Instead, unworkable action leads us to become stuck or experiencing increases in our struggles. Such actions may involve those that are reactive, impulsive, or automatic rather than being purposeful, considered, mindful actions that are motivated persistently by experiential avoidance instead of values. They may also include procrastination or inaction rather than effective action, to improve quality of life. Some common examples of unworkable action include social withdrawal, excessive use of alcohol or drugs, physical inactivity, avoiding work, excessive watching of television or sleeping, stopping activities that were previously enjoyable, procrastinating on important tasks, and even attempting suicide.

## Attachment to the conceptualised self

Each of us has our own story about who we are, which has many layers and is rather complex. Our story includes facts like our age, name, cultural background, sex, marital status, occupation and so forth. It also evaluates and describes different roles we play, our strengths and weaknesses, our hopes, aspirations, and dreams, the relationships we have, and our likes and dislikes. When we can lightly hold onto our story, we can develop a sense of self that is helpful in defining who we are and what it is we want in life. However, if we act as if we are the actual story itself by becoming fused with it, this then creates all kinds of problems. This is referred to as *self-as-description*, which is a way of describing ourselves. When we are fused with this self-description as if that description is who we are, it feels as though all the thoughts generated in this description are genuinely who we are.

## Overlap Among Pathological Processes

Just as with psychological flexibility, these pathological processes are all interconnected. If an individual is ruminating on why they think they are such a failure, this could be classed as self-as-description or fusion. If the person spends time ruminating and pacing up and down rather than taking action in a life-enhancing way, this could be classed as unworkable action. If the individual is caught up in their thoughts while in the company of other people, they are not only losing contact with the here and now, but likely losing contact with the values relating to engagement and connection with others. Such rumination may also function as experiential avoidance if it is done in a way that avoids thinking or having to deal with other painful issues, or trying to act as a distraction from feelings within themselves.

## A Further Step Yet

Acceptance and commitment therapy provides a sound, straightforward approach to being able to deal with unhelpful thoughts and feelings, and provides beneficial strategies for addressing the cognitive fusion that can result when we are psychologically inflexible. It is relatively easy to use and can have excellent results for those who adopt and practice its concepts. Using selected ACT strategies alongside those derived from positive psychology provides a firm framework for the creation and maintenance of healthy cognitions to enhance wellbeing.

However, in the case of the veterinary profession, as has been illustrated earlier, certain unique work stressors feature strongly as negative impacts on vet wellbeing. As a result, some young vets find their ideas of what the profession would be like day-to-day before they commenced work have not been met by reality. While it might be said this is a feature in many professions, the alarming rates of mental health distress in vets lends support to the vital importance of career choice questions when using interventions to increase vet wellbeing. Vets who may be questioning whether they would like to remain within the profession or not, or for those wondering if veterinary science is an appropriate career choice for them could thus benefit from the application of *career construction theory* in addition to the principles of positive psychology and ACT. Let's take a look at what this is about in the next chapter.

# Chapter 5

# Career Construction Theory

Career construction theory derives from the principles of individual differences psychology, developmental psychology, and narrative psychology. It grew out of Mark Savickas's work in 2001 which incorporated the earlier ideas of Donald Super from the 1950s. The theory proposes a model for understanding vocational behaviour across one's life-cycle and providing a way to comprehend how people use and choose work as well as providing practical skills to assist people in making vocational choices and maintaining satisfying work lives. Career construction theory helps to explain how individuals construct themselves through both inter-personal and interpretive processes.

There are said to be three perspectives of career construction theory on vocational behaviour, consisting of:

- the *differential* — this perspective looks at *what* the preferences are for different people, and is derived from the discipline of individual differences psychology,

- the *developmental* — this perspective examines *how* people cope with work traumas, vocational development tasks, and occupational transitions, and stems from developmental psychology, and

- the *dynamic* — this perspective considers *why* people distinctly fit work into their lives and derives from the narrative psychological perspective.

In addition to the *what, how,* and *why* of vocational behaviour, career construction theory further identifies *the self* as having three components.

- Self as actor (that is, identity/personality).

- Self as agent (that is, adaptability).

- Self as author (that is, stories/narratives).

The construction of a career is likened to that of *self-making*, and therefore, career construction theory focuses on forming and utilising a narrative about a career. First with the self as an *actor* (i.e. co-constructing person types and reputation), then later becoming *agents* who are directing the action (i.e. adapting to traumas, tasks, and transitions), and finally developing into *authors* who explain that action (i.e. narrating a career story).

Career construction theory states that careers are about mattering and that by imposing meaning on vocational behaviour, people build their careers. As such, there is an emphasis on the processes, both interpretive and interpersonally, through which people inflict direction and meaning on vocational behaviour.

From constructionist viewpoints on subjective careers, people put meaning on the memories of their past, identify experiences in the present, and consider their aspirations for the future. They are then able to intertwine them into such a way that then portrays a life theme or life story. The life theme or life story aspect of career construction theory considers the 'why' of vocational behaviour in relation to the subject matter of one's work life. It is said that such stories relating to an individual's career highlight the themes they use to make meaningful choices, and subsequently how they adjust to their work roles. Career construction theory seeks to be comprehensive by addressing the 'why' of life themes, together with the 'how' of career adaptability and the 'what' of personality.

The three central components of *life themes, vocational personality*, and *career adaptability* provide overall structure to the application of the theory.

## Life Themes

Stemming from the original early work by Super, this aspect of career construction theory addresses how individuals build their careers by imposing meaning on their vocational behaviour. Careers are about mattering, which is subsequently highlighted through life themes in the following ways.

- We turn our ideas of the type of person we are into 'occupational terminology' and then express our vocational preferences in such a way.

- We gain entry to an occupation and develop a self-concept.

- We stabilise ourselves with an occupation while subsequently identifying our potential — and in turn, preserving our self-esteem.

## Vocational Personality

Vocational personality can be referred to as the needs, interests, values, and career-related abilities that a person has. However, career construction theory suggests that other career-related traits and interests should not be categorised as traits or factors, rather, they should be viewed as *reputation* and *resemblances* to skills and attitudes that are socially constructed. As such, they have no measurable truth or reality value outside themselves, they do not reside within a person, nor can they be internally extracted through the use of interest inventories (which are commonly used in career guidance and assessment). It is believed that they are not stable traits capable of predicting the future; rather, they are relationship 'phenomena' that highlight socially constructed meanings.

## Career Adaptability

Viewing career construction as 'a series of attempts to implement a self-concept in social roles' highlights the importance of career adaptability. Throughout a person's working life they will face the need to adapt to a series of transitions — from school to work, from job to job, and from occupation to occupation. Additional to work, individuals must also adapt to the expectations of play and building relationships. Increasing career adaptability is a central goal of career construction counselling.

In career construction theory the various derivations of the root word 'adapt' (which in Latin means to join or fit), such as *adaptivity, adaptation,* and *adapting* indicate a sequence spanning across adaptation results, adaptability resources, adaptive readiness, and adapting responses. Adaptability can emphasise the processes a person uses to cope with constructing their career and connecting with their community, and there are suggestions that there are a set of specific attitudes, beliefs, and consequences which form the strategies for coping behaviours and problem-solving used by individuals to integrate their work roles with their vocational self-concept. These are known as the ABCs of career construction. In this regard, the ABCs can be further grouped into four dimensions of adaptability, namely: concern, control, curiosity, and confidence.

Figure 5.1 represents a visual perspective of career construction theory.

## Career Construction Theory in Action

The career counselling model for career construction provides a step-by-step interview process for the career counsellor to use the concepts of *construction, deconstruction, reconstruction, co-construction,* and *action.*

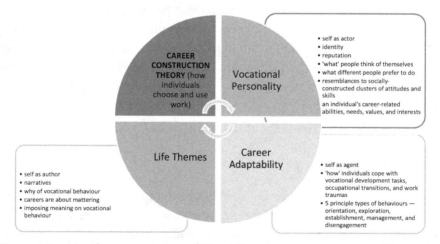

Figure 5.1.  Visual representation of the different components comprising career construction theory showing the aspects of vocational personality, life themes, and career adaptability.

## Construction

Firstly, the career construction counselling would start by having the individual describe the following:

- the event that detached them from the current chapter in their career story,

- the individual's adaptive resources and readiness, and

- the individual's aims for a new and different scenario that they wish to co-construct.

From the constructionist perspective, the career counsellor would then try to elicit vocational stories from the individual. This would likely be conducted as follows:

- Asking the individual about their role models (to examine how they have constructed themselves as *actor*).

- Rather than asking about inventoried interests, the counsellor would ask about manifest interests (to examine strivings and goals as *agent*), such as their favourite television shows or books and so forth.

- To examine the individual as *author*, the counsellor would ask the individual to detail a script from their favourite movie, story, or book.

- Asking the individual for a favourite saying, which normally indicates the adaptability resources and actions required in order to move to the next segment in the occupational plot.

- Finally, the counsellor would ask about the earliest recollection the individual can recall. While most individuals would recall their earliest recollection as a somewhat negative experience portraying a central conflict and motif, earliest recollections are more about what lies ahead (i.e., the future) in that the individual can select, elaborate and then reconstruct such memories to guide future or present action.

## Deconstruction

Throughout the career counselling interview, the counsellor listens for vignettes that need to be deconstructed, so any unrealistic or dominant ideas or expectations can be revealed and defeated in relation to their confining roles, self-limiting ideas, and cultural barriers. Many times, the vignettes requiring deconstruction are related to gender, race, or social class biases. Once these have been deconstructed, new pathways and choices may be possible in ways that have not previously been seen.

From the career counsellor's perspective, it is important to remember that the individual's stories are not determining the future but are an active attempt at the individual making meaning and shaping the future. When an individual tells their story, they are constructing a possible future.

## Reconstruction

From the individual's constructions of their work life, narratively processing vocational stories can assist in identifying important events and integrating them into a grand story about the career. The 'identity' narrative thus tells the story of an individual who becomes a person in a world they have co-constructed with their significant others. This portrayal places social mattering and personal meaning on an individual's life as it also tells about progress and patterns. However, this story highlights aspects of lived experience relevant to the questions the individual has asked, rather than telling a complete life story.

To avoid getting caught up or disoriented by the many events, complexities and contradictions of an individual's life, the career counsellor listens for the glue that holds these facts together, instead of just listening for the facts, as it is this theme that makes a 'whole' of the life.

## Co-construction

Once the career narrative has been reconstructed, the career counsellor presents a draft of the life portrait to the individual — including career themes, occupational plots, and character arcs. The individual is encouraged to edit the life portrait (which involves adjustments, alterations, and amendments), enabling them to make it more liveable and extending it into the future. This aspect is critical as it also predicts positive outcomes.

Once the intentions of the individual are clear to themselves and the counsellor, they are then ready to face the disruptions and challenges in their occupational plots, visualise the next scene, and commence action. Action is necessary to turn intentions into behaviour absorbed with meaning. The career counsellor and individual craft together an agenda of action to enable the individual to move from their current situation to the one they desire.

## One More Step

Because of certain unique aspects of daily work that are required within the veterinary profession, some vets, no matter what help they may seek to maintain their mental health, will question the basics of their career choice. It is important therefore to consider the involvement of career construction counselling in the training of vets as well as through their early career experiences. For established working vets any wellbeing intervention should also include aspects of career construction theory to ensure a vet's past career stories do not determine their future. Instead, they can be used to shape the future through destabilising demoralising stories and reconstructing a life portrait. Learning practical skills through an understanding of one's vocational behaviour can turn tension into intention, leading to a more satisfying life.

So, having looked at the contributions that positive psychology, ACT, and career construction theory can make to the mental health and wellbeing of vets, we come to a final step before bringing it all together — building a resilient mindset. Let's take a look at what this is about in the next chapter.

# Chapter 6

# Resilience

What do you think about when you think of resilience? Do you think of resilience as the ability to bounce back after every setback? Or do you think of resilience as being able to keep powering through the day no matter what life throws at you? Or do you think of something else altogether?

Individuals who are resilient are said to be those who encompass a set of attitudes or assumptions about themselves that have an influence on their developing skills and behaviours. These behaviours and skills influence the assumptions we have, so there is a constantly-operating dynamic process. This set of assumptions is referred to as a mindset. Therefore, an individual with a resilient mindset is said to have several main characteristics:

- Feeling as though they have control of their life.

- Possessing and being a person with empathy.

- Knowing how to strengthen their hardiness for stress.

- Exhibiting interpersonal capability and effective communication.

- Learning from failure and success.

- Forming realistic expectations and goals.

- Having solid decision-making and problem-solving skills.

- Living life responsibly based on thoughtful values.

- Acting as a contributing and compassionate society member.

- Helping others to feel special, while feeling special themselves.

Resilience can also be described as the ability to bounce back, and while it is closely related to tough-mindedness, it is not the same thing. Whereas tough-mindedness can incorporate qualities such as being strong-willed, determined, or even avoiding seeing situations through the eyes of others, resilience can be found in both the brashest people and the quietest people.

The term resilience is also used to measure a community's capacity to rebuild itself following a natural catastrophe, some of which may involve starvation and extreme deprivation, as well as how soon the restoration of services occurs. It can also be referred to as a term for communities who can redefine themselves following downturns such as the disappearance of traditional industries. Resilience can also be more about how you bounce back or respond to events in your life, rather than what actually happens to you at the time of the event, and is about establishing a level of acceptance and flexibility in relation to life events. The good news is that resilience is not necessarily only gained by experiencing some unfortunate event — it is possible to create psychological fortitude and strength by undergoing events that are positive as well. While being in possession of a resilient mindset does not infer that a person is free from conflict, stress, and pressure, it can imply, however, that they are able to successfully cope with problems as they surface.

When we look at resilience, we can also look at both positive and negative scripts. A positive script is when a behaviour that leads to positive outcomes is repeated, however, on the opposite end are behaviours that are self-defeating, or counterproductive, which, if continually repeated, will result in a negative script developing. Such negative scripts are obstacles to the development of a resilient mindset.

It seems that some people have a genetic influence of resilience — when faced with separation or grief, some people have the ability to naturally resume their former mental shape without disconnection, while there are others who seemingly spend most of their lives trying to find their peace of mind and lost confidence. Interestingly, military psychologists working with those who have post-traumatic stress disorder (PTSD) have discovered there are some people who are more predisposed to states triggered by events that create high-stress, hyper-attentiveness, and anxiety, while others seemingly have less long-term effects.

The negative events we experience in our lives can be life-changing, terrible, painful, and soul-destroying, and may last for some time. However, these events do not have to tarnish the rest of our lives, as often such things can materialise as learning experiences which can gift us with wisdom if we are prepared to use these encounters as experiences from which we can learn and grow. It is important to note, however, that this does not imply we should forget these events, rather, we should aim to reflect and learn on such events instead of becoming stuck or fused to them.

When we can accept that our life is going to involve a mixed bag of experiences that will be both positive and negative, it places us in a much better position to be able to deal with the life events that will undoubtedly be thrown at us from time to time. Being able to accept the things we can and cannot change in our life can be one of the most important factors in being able to understand resilience. Essentially this means accepting and learning not to put our energy and focus into the things that are not working so well for us, but instead being able to grow and work with the things that are right in our lives.

Being able to develop the virtue of patience, by solving problems and breaking them down into smaller, more manageable pieces, is key to building resilience. So too is the ability to cultivate a sense of self-compassion for yourself and the experiences you have encountered. This involves being kind and gentle with yourself, as well as undertaking pleasant personal activities such as helping others, eating well, exercising, and meditating.

Interestingly, the founder of positive psychology, Martin Seligman, describes how the United States army used training in emotional resilience, and how resilience has been revealed to be a protective factor for soldiers going to war. That is, when research was conducted into why some soldiers came back from war suffering post-traumatic stress disorder and others did not, it was discovered those not suffering post-traumatic stress disorder had higher levels of resilience. Encouragingly, according to Seligman, resilience (as well as optimism) can be learned.

## Keys for a Resilient Life

Psychologists Robert Brooks and Sam Goldstein have written extensively on resilience in both children and adults. I find their ten keys for living resiliently helpful in my daily practice. They are summarised below as a guide to developing and maintaining a resilient mindset.

### Rewriting your negative scripts and changing the words of life

There is an assumption that people can shift from negative ways of feeling, thinking, and behaving, to more positive behaviours that are consistent with a resilient mindset. By following a sequence of steps, there can be provision for a change in direction — albeit that such change may take time depending upon how frequently and how long the negative script has been used, as well as the openness to change, the ability to effectively handle obstacles, and the awareness of the negative script.

The recommended steps in this sequence are listed below.

- Rather than expecting other people to change, identify your own negative scripts and take responsibility for changing them.

- Look at the issue at hand and define both short- and long-term goals relative to this issue.

- Be open to the possibility of new plans of action or scripts that are aligned with your goals.

- List the criteria for assessing your new script's success and select the script you feel will afford you the greatest chance of success.

- Predict any potential obstacles that could block your success and reflect on how these could be managed.

- Implement the new script you have chosen and measure its effectiveness.

- If the course of action you have chosen is proven to be unsuccessful, change your goals or scripts accordingly.

## Rather than a stressed-out path, choose one that is stress-hardy

Being able to manage pressure and stress is a basic characteristic found in resilient people. One's life experiences, together with an inborn temperament, play a contributing role in why some people seem to live a more stressful existence than do others. Interestingly, it has been found that some people are in fact predisposed to feeling more intense stress than others.

## View life through the eyes of other people

Resilient people have satisfying relationships, and at the core of these relationships is the ability to see things from the perspective of other people, or, that is, the capacity to be empathic. Empathy has been shown to be an important feature of emotional intelligence, and there are studies alluding to the fact that empathy can be learned.

## Practice effective communication

Linked closely to empathy is the ability to effectively communicate with others, which is a core part of resilience. Being able to communicate effectively includes the ability for active listening, together with understanding how both our nonverbal and verbal messages are perceived by others. When we participate in active listening, we endeavour to validate and understand what is being communicated to us by other people. Validation, however, does not denote agreement but instead indicates we can understand without being demeaning.

## Accept others as well as yourself

It is essential that we learn how to accept ourselves if we are to cultivate a mindset that is resilient. When we practice acceptance, we imply that we have goals and expectations that are realistic, we lead a balanced and authentic life where our values, goals, and behaviours are in alignment, and we also recognise our vulnerabilities and our strengths. Unauthentic people are likely to experience an increased level of pressure and stress when their actions are not aligned with their values. Unfortunately, many people get so caught up in the hassles of everyday life that they have no awareness that there is a discrepancy between their values, goals, and behaviour. Such discrepancies can act as major barriers to leading a life that is fulfilling and with integrity.

### Display compassion and make connections

There has been much literature over the past few years documenting how important it is to feel connected to others in order to have a sense of resilience and emotional wellbeing. Even in adulthood — irrespective of our sense of confidence or security — it is important for us to have charismatic adults in our lives who we continually gather strength from.

### Effectively deal with mistakes

Another essential component of a resilient mindset is the way in which we respond to, and understand, our failures and mistakes. People who are resilient generally see these things as opportunities for learning and growth. While this does not equate to them being ecstatic when they experience mistakes, it does indicate they look for opportunities that could be a by-product of such setbacks, rather than not being discouraged. In comparison, those without such resilience regularly interpret these mistakes as 'proof' they are a failure. Their attribution to mistakes tends to be related to conditions that cannot be corrected easily, such as a lack of intelligence, and they tend to become reliant on coping behaviours that are self-defeating, or quitting, denying, avoiding things, or placing blame on other people.

### Build masses of competence by dealing well with success

The way an individual reacts to their successes in life is just as important as the way in which they respond to, and understand, setbacks if they are to maintain a resilient mindset. Just like altering a mindset that is negative in relation to mistakes we make, it is also possible to put into motion a more positive and empowering mindset with regard to the achievements we make.

### Develop self-control and self-discipline

Playing a significant role in our day-to-day activities are self-control and self-discipline. When we demonstrate empathy by thinking before we act and are considerate of other's feelings, when we consider certain solutions to problems, when we stop ourselves from yelling at someone whose actions have made us feel angry, or when we respond in thoughtful and rational ways, we are displaying self-control and self-discipline.

## Maintain a resilient lifestyle

When considering a lifestyle that enables us to maintain resilience, we must adopt the same principles we would if we were to abandon our well-established exercise programs and diets. If we were to abandon these things, it is inevitable that our health will suffer. Therefore, adopting healthy diets, exercise programs, and a resilient mindset necessitate these aspects becoming a way of life. We cannot just assume that once these aspects are developed that they will maintain themselves, as without doubt there will always be unexpected and expected challenges that materialise which will test our resilience. Having a good sense of the characteristics of people who are resilient, and being able to participate in such exercises daily, will assist us in maintaining and strengthening a long-term resilient mindset.

# SECTION FOUR

# Intervention

# The Coping and Wellbeing Program for Veterinary Professionals

## Introduction

O kay, so now you've read about some of the major impacts around working in the veterinary profession, it's time to do something about it!

This section covers the core subjects from the *Complete Coping and Wellbeing Program for Veterinary Professionals* which is offered as a one-or two-day workshop to help you to:

- feel less-stressed and able to proactively manage stress the healthy way,

- build and maintain wellbeing and quality of life with positive psychology,

- easily deal with unhelpful thoughts and feelings that run rampant inside your head and body,

- become more resilient,

- be better organised and in control of your time,

- get your message across confidently and assertively,

- feel calmer, more relaxed, and balanced, and

- achieve your goals.

The topics we will address in the program include:

- stress-management tips,

- time-management tips,

- communication and assertiveness strategies,

- relaxation strategies,

- SMART goal setting,

- acceptance and commitment therapy, and

- positive psychology.

The strategies are grouped into 7 modules. You don't have to run through all modules sequentially and indeed you might like to dive straight into a particular module that interests you or you feel is most appropriate right now. No matter what approach you use please take your time to read through all the strategies and make notes as you go. Try to explicitly implement at least one strategy every day and note what difference it makes on how you feel. Make sure you keep on trying the strategies — they won't work if you don't apply them!

You'll find some fill-in lists and action sheets for your use with some of the module strategies. If you'd rather not write in this book, or need more room, simply photocopy them or draw up your own.

If you feel you or a colleague need something to help that is more in-depth than this self-help program you can access a more comprehensive version by attending a workshop.

Check out www.positivepsychsolutions.com.au for more information.

Remember too that if you feel overwhelmed by stress or worry at any time you should seek professional assistance. Contact details to help you find a registered psychologist in your area can usually be found online via the professional body for the profession. For example in Australia that is the *Australian Psychological Society*, in the UK the *British Psychological Association* and in the US, the *American Psychological Association*. You should also talk to your regular doctor about an appropriate professional to help you or if your need is immediate seek the assistance of reputable prominent helplines. Remember, asking for help when you need it shows the wisdom of knowing and accepting yourself and confidence in your decisions.

# Module 1

# Stress Management

Did you know there is 'good' stress (called 'eustress') as well as 'bad' stress (called 'distress')? We need a certain amount of both the good and the bad stress, as this is what helps to keep us motivated.

For example, if you are getting a bit tense and irritable about getting your suitcase packed and getting to the airport on time for a 9.00am flight, you may be feeling quite stressed. But once you are on that plane and en route to your destination, that stress generally disappears — this is an example of eustress. If you weren't feeling this level of stress, you may not have the same motivation or sense of urgency to get things going and keep you on track for getting to the airport on time. However, on the flip side, if you were running around in a state of panic and feeling completely overwhelmed and out of control in this situation, this clearly would not be helpful and would be more attuned to distress!

Ultimately, stress can have fatal consequences, so being able to effectively manage our stress is vital for our health and wellbeing. Let's look at a **top ten list of stress busting strategies** that you can start using right now.

# Stress Busting List

### 1.   Know your stressors

Learn to recognise the things that get you stressed (your 'stressors'). For example, if you know that catching a train full of crowded people to go to a concert where you'll be in the mosh pit is going to get you totally stressed out, then consider if it is really a good idea. If you really want to attend the concert and travel by train, then develop appropriate strategies for helping you to acknowledge that you will likely be feeling stressed, and how you can effectively cope with this (see step 9).

### 2.   Recognise your symptoms

Being able to recognise the symptoms you feel when you are stressed (such as things like a tense stomach, feeling nauseous, being irritable and short-tempered, breathing more rapidly, sweating, and having an increased heart rate) can help you take a more proactive role in combating stress. If you recognise the symptoms early on, you can become more proactive in dealing with them.

### 3.   Practice mindfulness

Mindfulness is essentially about 'being in the moment' or the 'here and now'. When you are mindful, you are not caught up in the past or future – you are dealing with this very moment, right here, right now. Right now is the only moment you can respond to your present thoughts and feelings, so when you are able to recognise them as they are happening, you can take steps to ensure your behaviour is aligned with your values to get a better outcome in the long run. One quick and easy mindfulness strategy is to 'just notice' – just notice 5 things you can see, hear, feel, taste, touch, and smell. This brings you back into the current moment, where you can then take action.

## 4. Relaxation

Relaxation isn't just about sitting down and doing nothing! Relaxation is whatever you do that helps you to feel relaxed — so for some people this could be different things. Some common forms of relaxation include meditation, surfing, gardening, dancing, reading, art, singing, different forms of exercising, stroking an animal, listening to music, watching TV, colouring in, journalling, reflecting, laughing, and sitting quietly.

## 5. Socialisation

For many people, surrounding ourselves with supportive friends and family can be a great form of stress relief. Laughing releases endorphins (the feel-good chemicals) and helps us to de-stress in the long run. Being with family and friends can also distract us from whatever our minds are caught up in, and help us to focus on something else in the short term.

## 6. Work/life balance

Developing a good work-life balance is essential to our health and wellbeing. Despite popular beliefs, work-life balance is not about spending 50% of our time at work, and 50% of our time at home! It is about finding a BALANCE that works for us — so for some people it might be 60–40 or 70–30 — whatever works for us that allows us to spread our time between the demands of work and life, but also making sure we have time for relaxation and leisure!

### 7. Set SMART goals

Sometimes we can get stressed because we do not have SMART goals. SMART goals are specific, measurable, achievable, realistic, and time-based. When our goals are SMART, we are in a much better position to achieve them as they are more likely to be realistic. Make sure that you do not place too many expectations on yourself that you will not be able to meet, as this can create additional stress, and affect self-esteem and confidence.

### 8. Learn assertiveness skills

Learn how to speak up and say no! For some of us, we get stressed because we do not know how to say no effectively, and then feel resentful because we are lumbered with all these things that we didn't want! When you are assertive, you are able to get your message across in a respectful manner — being respectful to yourself and the other person. Being assertive is NOT about being aggressive or passive — it is about confidently and respectfully taking ownership of how you are feeling when a particular thing happens by making 'I' statements, and stating what you would like as the outcome.

### 9. Develop appropriate coping strategies

Stress is a very real part of life for all of us. What stresses one person is not necessarily going to stress another person, and therefore we are all going to experience stress in different ways. Being able to develop APPROPRIATE coping strategies is essential to managing stress and enabling us to keep a sense of well-being. I recommend strategies such as acceptance and commitment therapy, and positive psychology.

## 10.  Seek professional help

If you feel like stress has control of you, it is essential to take appropriate action and do something about it. Being proactive rather than reactive is crucial! If you do not feel like you have appropriate strategies (and by this, I mean healthy, legal, and safe!), I highly recommend you seek professional help. Speaking with your GP or psychologist is a great way of taking action, as they can generally help you to develop your own appropriate coping strategies to combat stress.

# Module 2

# Time Management

Even when your working day is structured around client appointments during which you can try to keep as time efficient as possible by doing your job efficiently and professionally, there are many non-client contact hours that also need to be managed. I am naturally a very organised person (which has helped me enormously during my years working full-time, studying, and raising a family!), but appreciate that not everyone shares the same level of time management. Here are some of the best time-management strategies I have found — many of them which I use personally.

### De-cluttering / Mind Dumping

If you think of your mind as a drawer or bookshelf — there is only so much information that can be stored in there at any one time. Once that drawer or bookshelf is full, there is no room left for anything else to be stored there — if we try to cram more in, it will eventually collapse or give way.

Sometimes there are so many competing demands on our minds that it all becomes very overwhelming and we feel as though we can no longer cope. Therefore it is essential that we are able to empty out

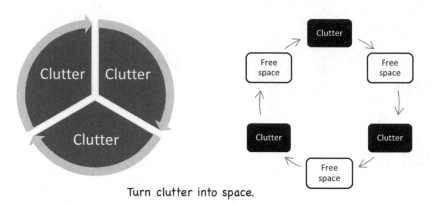

**Turn clutter into space.**

information in order to make way for new information to fit. When we have a nice balance with this, information is able to come and go more freely.

### ✅ Mind Dump Action Sheet

Prepare a list of all the things going on in your mind right now, to enable you to start to declutter:

1. _____

2. _____

3. _____

4. _____

5. _____

. . .

## Make a 'to-do' list

Making a to-do list or list of tasks is a great way to get all those thoughts in your head down on paper — where you can stop having to try and remember them all!

Make a complete list of all the tasks (both large and small) that are running around in your head. This list should include things like projects, work tasks — emails, phone calls, reports, meetings, follow-ups, calendar items, social requests, family commitments, appointments, etc. Some tasks you are thinking about may not yet be well formed — for example you know that you feel pressured about banking some undeposited cheques when you normally receive payments via card facilities and are unsure when you can get the time to duck out. Don't spend time trying to plan an action then and there, just write 'bank' on your list as a prompt so that you know the thought won't be lost again in a busy day.

As soon as you think you have written down everything to go on the list, take a break, continue your day, then revisit the list at the end of day. You might find more items to add. Complete this, making any changes to each entry where necessary and try to allocate a due date for each of those tasks.

### To-Do List

Prepare a list of all the tasks you need to do and when they need to be done by:

| Task | Date due by |
|------|-------------|
| 1. _____ | _____ |
| 2. _____ | _____ |
| 3. _____ | _____ |

4. _____    _____

5. _____    _____

...

## Set up a 'Tickler' file

Tickler files are like mini-reminders. They act as prompts, so anything in that particular file is a reminder that you have to do something that day or within that month.

You set up a 'tickler' file by having one file for each day of the month (so they would be labelled 1–30/31) or one file for each month (January to December). Using your 'to-do' list, go through the allocated dates you made for each entry on when it is required, and then transfer all the items for each particular day or month onto another list and place that with any relevant paperwork in its appropriate tickler file. This is particularly helpful for invoices payable.

Having a tickler file eliminates the need to have to check and re-check through your to-do list each day to see if you've missed a deadline on something or rifle through multiple clusters of documents sitting on your desk. Instead, you open the relevant day's file and address each of the items in it. This means you can stop worrying about trying to get everything accomplished in one day, by allowing you to prioritise things that are really important TODAY.

## Clear or tidy your desk

For many of us, when our desks and offices or homes are cluttered, our minds feel cluttered. Being able to clear away this clutter allows us some clarity and focus.

Completely clear your desk. If an item requires action, decide when you will act on it, write it on the document, and put it in your tickler file. If something needs filing, mark it 'filing' and put it in a filing tray/folder. If something needs to be on someone else's desk — put it there. Remember, if in doubt, throw it out!

If something lands on your desk that would take less than two minutes to complete, such as signing a basic form or okaying an account transaction, do it immediately and get the paperwork off the desk to where it needs to go next.

## On the phone

While it is of course not possible to predict when the phone will ring you should certainly group important phone calls together and do them all at once. To keep them as concise as possible, plan ahead of your scheduled calls by, for example, making a list of questions you need to ask and keep that list next to you through the phone call, checking off the questions when completed.

Despite how busy and pressured you may feel when someone rings unexpectedly, focus your concentration on the call. Resist the temptation to check your emails at the same time, or to keep tapping at your keyboard. Multitasking always involves a trade-off of cognitive effort between tasks and reduces the effectiveness of both. Instead, try standing up from your desk while talking. This will help you focus on the call, is good for physical health, and sends a non-verbal message that you are time limited for this task.

## Your Personal Prime Time

Not every hour in a day is as effective as it can be at work. Concentration wanes over time, daily body rhythms vary. It is important therefore to learn about your personal prime time.

To do this, using the action sheet design below as a guide split your day into 2-hour time segments. Then keep this handy as you work through a typical day. Put an 'x' into the appropriate 2-hour time segment box to indicate how your level of energy is travelling over time.

Once you have completed the chart with x's, a typical day can be graphed by connecting the x's to see how and where each day has its ups and downs (with 'ups' showing as more to the right on the graph). Where there are times of high energy, pick that particular time segment as your prime time, which is when you are at your peak mentally or physically.

Once you have identified your prime time, there are three things you need to do:

- Respect this time. Do not do trivial tasks such as filing, tidying your desk, etc., as you are potentially putting off starting a difficult task. Try to stay on track by disciplining yourself.

- Protect your prime time. Block the 2-hour period off on your calendar so activities of less importance don't impede this time.

- Direct your prime time. Schedule the tasks requiring the most concentration and energy (and generally the most important ones) into this part of your day.

## ☑ Personal Prime-Time Action Sheet

Tick or cross next to each time segment indicating the level to which you feel you are active or motivated. Plan to use this as your most 'productive' time within the day to try and get as many of your activities completed as possible.

You can also use this table to plan or schedule activities within each of the time segments.

| Time Block | Energy Level (1 = low, 5 = high) | | | | |
|---|---|---|---|---|---|
| | 1 | 2 | 3 | 4 | 5 |
| 06.00am–08.00am | | | | | |
| 08.00am–10.00am | | | | | |
| 10.00am–12.00pm | | | | | |
| 12.00pm–02.00pm | | | | | |
| 02.00pm–04.00pm | | | | | |
| 04.00pm–06.00pm | | | | | |
| 06.00pm–08.00pm | | | | | |
| 08.00pm–10.00pm | | | | | |
| 10.00pm–12.00am | | | | | |
| 12.00am–02.00am | | | | | |
| 02.00am–04.00am | | | | | |
| 04.00am–06.00am | | | | | |

## The most important 15 minutes of your day

It can take just 15 minutes to schedule your entire work day. Therefore, you should block off 15 minutes on your calendar each day and use this time to make sure your days are ones of purpose, direction, meaning, and accomplishment.

It is recommended that you undertake this 15-minute schedule at the end of your workday in order to make your momentum work for you (ideas are generally fresher at the end of each day, as you have an awareness of what you achieved or did not achieve that day). By doing this at the end of the workday, it gives you a sense of closure on the day and also enables you to identify the most important tasks to do the next day, giving you the opportunity to start the task first thing the next morning.

## Calendars and diaries

Keep an appointment calendar, and make sure you put everything into it. Keep a time inventory or schedule (e.g. 8.30am – 9.30am: respond to emails).

Rank your priorities:

A = urgent

B = important

C = no time frame

Then itemise each one in each category as A1, A2, etc., to list each urgent item and its priority. For example, A1 would mean it would need to be attended to before anything else.

## Procrastination List

We all procrastinate over some things. There are numerous reasons for this, but it is important nonetheless that we try and reduce our personal procrastination list to as small as possible. Try making a list of all the things you have been procrastinating about lately. Rate each of these items in terms of how much pressure you feel for not having completed them. Start with the item that has been bothering you the most and do it now! Continue down your list until everything has been completed. Start working through the list as soon as you can. Don't procrastinate about it!

 **Procrastination List**

Prepare a list of all the things you know you are currently procrastinating about:

1. _____

2. _____

3. _____

4. _____

5. _____

...

## Handling visitors

For consulting practice vets or those involved in other areas of the industry, the times when you need to work at your desk aren't always free of interruptions from visitors. In these cases you cannot simply be rude or inattentive as this conveys a very unprofessional demeanour and ultimately can harm your reputation. Instead, to reduce the time these visits take from your work where possible meet visitors outside your office or if in your office stand up and confer so they don't get too comfortable. Try and set time limits (e.g., 'I have a phone call to return in 5 minutes'). You might even develop some 'rescue signals' with co-workers to cut an unarranged meeting short.

## Handling internal drop-ins

Of course, not all visitors to your desk will come from outside your place of work. Meetings with one's coworkers, both professional and friendly, are an inevitable and important part of working life. But there is no reason you cannot also ensure these are manageable and do not cause you stress. Regular short catch ups with associates and coworkers limit the need for more time-costly meetings. It is also important to agree on a 'quiet time' for such catch ups when there are fewer other demands on your time (e.g. client bookings) and to ensure you establish such times when you are available to others. Finally, when making time for others at your work, make sure you block interruptions (e.g. text/phone calls and email notifications) to get the most out of your time.

## Cluster your time

Wherever possible, set aside a designated time period where you can cluster similar activities together – for example, emails and phone calls.

## General tips

- Each morning, do the most important item first.

- Realign your levels of stress by looking out the window, taking a walk outside, or changing your mindset.

- If you have any 'in-between' time, (e.g. waiting for someone to get back to you, or you have 10 minutes to 'burn' before an appointment), use this time effectively, such as: returning phone calls, keeping a file with reading material in it and read something out of it, clean your desk and put things back in their proper places, go through your daily action list, update your daily action lists and waiting lists, check your mail, write a note or memo.

## Putting it all together — time to take action now!

- Prepare your 'mind dump'.

- Identify your 'to-do' list.

- Prioritise items on your 'to-do' list.

- Complete your personal prime time chart.

- Prepare an appointment calendar/diary.

- Prepare your procrastination list.

# Module 3

# Communication and Assertiveness

I am a firm believer that communication is at the core of so many problems in our day-to-day lives. Think about how many conversations are misconstrued, or how many people misinterpret a text message or email. In my private practice I have worked with a lot of couples undergoing relationship counselling. The majority of these couples had lost touch with how to communicate with each other either assertively, respectively, or both. Some of them wouldn't communicate at all, which often exacerbated the problem as this could lead to all sorts of scenarios in the other partner's mind!

It is therefore very important to your mental wellbeing to use assertive communication in both your workplace and at home – basically anywhere communication is required.

So, what exactly is communication all about?

There are three main types of communication:

- verbal (speech)

- non-verbal (e.g. facial expressions, body language, gestures)

- written (texts, emails, social media)

## Verbal Communication

Verbal communication is that which is spoken — it includes things such as:

- conversations with people that are face to face or via telephone,

- listening to things such as television or radio, or

- conversations through media such as FaceTime, Skype, Zoom, etc.

Using verbal communication is a way to communicate your ideas and thoughts using words, or in turn to listen to the words being spoken. While this communication is occurring, you need to be mindful of how your language is also expressing both *connotation* and *denotation*.

Connotation in verbal communication refers to the subjective or emotional meaning of words being used when someone is expressing themselves, rather than the denotation — the objective accepted dictionary meaning. As an example, you might talk about 'change' in a family's normal routine as a possible cause for the onset of new behaviour in a pet. This would be a normal and helpful step in trying to solve a client issue, however the client, due to their own unique experiences may attach negative emotions to the word 'change'. This might result in the client reacting in a defensive way when in fact there is no intention to be accusative or confronting in any way.

## Non-verbal Communication

Non-verbal communication involves all the other cues that come about within spoken communication. Since we do not robotically enunciate words from a fixed speaker these non-verbal cues are a significant part of communication. Non-verbal communication includes:

- gestures and facial expressions,

- how we present ourselves,

- body language,

- behaviour, and

- sign language.

Non-verbal communication gives you the opportunity to communicate attitudes, emotions, and affect, but it is important not to make assumptions about the connotation behind the message when you are interpreting it.

Non-verbal communication adds a layer of complexity to verbal communication in the following ways.

- It may contradict verbal messages (e.g. saying 'I'm fine' but the body language shows otherwise).

- It can be ambiguous (e.g. raising eyebrows or shrugging shoulders can send different messages).

- It conveys emotion (e.g. touching someone's arm or facial expressions such as smiling).

- It is multi-channelled (e.g. facials, voice, tone, body language).

When you think about different ways of communicating non-verbally, it is important to consider the ways in which your message could be interpreted. As an example, consider the statement 'how are you!'. Based on this sentence, you could interpret this a few ways — the first is that the sender may not have heard from you in a while and could be asking excitedly 'OMG how are you!', or it could be interpreted as something a little cranky like 'hmmm, so how are you!'.

The way we communicate non-verbally is obviously crucial, as it can be very easy for our message to be misconstrued. It is important to note how you are feeling while communicating to ensure you are being as congruent as you can. If you are stressed or pressured about a matter unrelated to the communication you are having you need to try and not let that intrude on your non-verbal signals. Try and stay in the moment. Giving a simple instruction to a staff member after being blindsided by a client complaining about the cost of treatment for their pet can quickly become loaded with inappropriate emotion unless you have given yourself time (and few deep breaths) to regather your focus.

Similarly, when listening to someone while our body language conveys that we need to be somewhere else will likely be noticed and interpreted in a way we are not in control of.

## Written Communication

Not so long ago, people wrote letters to each other as the main way to stay in contact for either friendship or business. Nowadays we tend to think that written communication is mostly about formal communication (excluding notes passed around class). Yet much more casual communication between friends, family, colleagues and even clients occur in a written context via texts, tweets, message services and emails, even though in our minds we are 'speaking' to the other person. The use of acronyms and emojis with a shared understanding of their meaning helps convey emotional content along with the words but can only go so far. Without even the complexities of a voice to convey extra meaning a quick typed text remains limited in the amount of subjective emotional content it can convey to the recipient.

Therefore, it is important to ensure you double-check anything you send BEFORE you send it, to make sure your communication is interpreted in the manner which it is intended (as best you can).

### ☑ Checking your written communication

Next time you compose an email to a colleague you do not see that often or a client, read the words to yourself before you send it while imagining you are speaking to them in person in a sarcastic or angry tone. Next, read the email again as if you were excitedly talking to your best friend. See if the message behind the words is still the same as you first intended.

## Poor Communication

In my experience there are three common forms of poor communication that most often cause difficulties both at home and at work. It is important to see if you identify with any of these as either something you might be prone to doing or something you recognise in someone you regularly communicate with.

### Passive communication

Sometimes people may behave in a passive manner because they have low self-esteem, limited levels of confidence, or low self-respect. They may feel that they do not have the right to say something or feel a certain way, or could even have the belief that no-one will listen to them and therefore there is little point in speaking up. Passive people will generally shy away from conversations, or look away, or say things like 'it doesn't matter', or 'it's not important', and may be very quiet, timid, and/or shy.

### Passive-aggressive communication

There are some people who act in a passive-aggressive way — this is where they may act both passively and aggressively at the same time. That is, they may act in an aggressive way by looking away, while at the same time making a loud 'huff' or muttering something under their breath. Passive-aggressive people do not come straight out with aggressive behaviour, rather, it is conducted in a more subtle way. They may choose to do this for a number of reasons — for example, they may wish to avoid confrontation by getting embroiled in a heated conversation, or they may feel their comments will not be listened to, or they may not feel confident enough to speak up directly.

### Aggressive communication

Aggressive people behave in a way that attempts to make others agree with them while having no regard for the other person's feelings or opinion. They tend to express their opinions and feelings in a manner that can be perceived as intimidating or bullying, or in a way that attacks other people who may be communicating at the time. Underneath this behaviour tends to be the desire to 'win' and force other people to accept their viewpoint regardless.

## Assertiveness

Although many people may think assertiveness and aggressiveness are the same thing, they are not – and you certainly do not need to be aggressive to be assertive.

People who are assertive say what they would like to say, and/or express themselves in a manner that is respectful to themselves and the other person/people. Assertive communication is the best way to communicate with others in difficult conversations, as it attempts to maintain a collaborative and positive approach to the discussion/s.

When acting in an assertive manner, you should maintain eye contact and ensure your body language is upright and confident (rather than slouched) to portray an image of confidence and assertiveness. You should always use 'I' statements rather than using accusatory comments (such as 'you did this' or 'you did that'), as this is an indication that you are taking responsibility for your own feelings, rather than blaming or accusing the other person. It also helps to reduce any potential retaliation from the other person, who is less likely to feel like they are being accused of something and less likely to respond defensively.

☑ **Assertiveness in action**

It is a disappointing fact that most vets will come across a client who feels it is okay to make snide remarks about the 'fancy car' you drive, or 'being out on your boat all day', because they have the misguided belief that you must be making heaps of money because of what you charge for your services. They may even get a little aggressive and accuse you of not 'really' caring about their animal otherwise you wouldn't consider the costs to your own practice. How would you deal with them assertively?

It might sound something like this:

> 'I feel that your comments towards me are very unfair, and untrue. Our services do cost money because the equipment, products, and running costs of operating our clinic are expensive to maintain. Unfortunately we do not receive any subsidies for our services, and I can understand how this may make them seem expensive in comparison to our (human) medical care. I'd be happy to discuss what services are available for your budget, but would appreciate it if you could please refrain from making these kinds of comments as they really do hurt me and are not true.'

When communicating assertively, it is good to say how you feel, state what the problem is, and then state how you would like the situation to be resolved. Again, don't forget to replace 'you' with 'I' to take responsibility for your feelings and to remove any accusatory comments that could result in resentment and defensive behaviour.

## Some helpful communication skills

In addition to what has been covered so far, there are a few advanced skills you can use to ensure your communication is the best it can be:

- Reframing

- Challenging

- Probing

## Reframing

Reframing is a way of putting things into a different perspective for someone. As an example, someone may be trying to lose weight and end up having a piece of chocolate cake. They could then say 'see I'm hopeless, I just ate that piece of cake and have blown it now!'.

If you were to reframe this scenario, you might reassure them that it is only one piece of cake and it really doesn't mean they have 'blown it', as it could be that they have managed to be cake free all week up-until that moment! It is a strategy to turn a negative into something positive by reframing their unhelpful perspective.

## Challenging

Sometimes we might need to challenge someone who seems to be unable to move forward. We might also like to think of challenging as a way of 'caring confrontation' — a way to confront or challenge someone in a caring and respectful manner.

You might use challenging with someone who keeps letting you down, or says one thing and then does not carry through with it, or does something completely different. For example, you may have a friend that says 'we'll go fishing this weekend', and then they cancel the day before you are due to go. If this is a continual pattern, you might then challenge your friend. For example: 'Hey Bob, I noticed you keep saying you want to go fishing with me every weekend, but then you cancel right before we are due to leave. I was wondering if there is something else going on that you don't want to tell me about?'.

## Probing

If you would like to know more about something (and aren't just being nosy!), probing is a technique you can use to help you delve a little deeper. However, please bear in mind this is something that should be done respectfully, and with consideration for the other person's feelings. You also need to be mindful that they may not wish to elaborate on things, and will need to know when to take a step back and stop probing.

When using probing, you use open-ended questions (i.e. those requiring more than a 'yes' or 'no' answer). So, imagine a friend says they are feeling upset about something — you might ask them (via probing) what or who has made them upset, or what happened to make them so upset.

## Module 4

# Relaxation

Relaxation is an important part of our health and wellbeing. We need to be able to relax to keep our stress and anxiety levels at a manageable level. It is important to realise that relaxation isn't just about sitting quietly and doing nothing (although some people do find this relaxing!). I like to think of relaxation essentially being about what makes you feel relaxed and helps you to get that wonderful feeling of 'calm' (of course, with my proviso that it needs to be safe, healthy, and legal!). What matters most then in looking at relaxation is to find out what sort of relaxation will suit you best.

It is important therefore if you try a relaxation activity that seems to be too difficult to achieve in a busy week or doesn't seem to be effective that you try something else.

 **Finding the relaxation activity that's best for you**

There are many different forms of relaxation. Read through the list below and mark out of 5 how relaxing you would find these. Add some extra ones if required. Choose the highest scoring three activities and try each of them to see how effective they are for you.

sitting quietly and deep breathing ————————

listening to music ————————————

yoga ——————————————

meditating ——————————————

dancing ——————————————

gardening ——————————————

walking ——————————————

jogging ——————————————

surfing ——————————————

playing a sport ——————————————

going to the gym ——————————————

other forms of exercise ——————————————

arts and crafts (including colouring-in!) ————————

sitting at the beach and watching the ocean ————

bushwalking ——————————————

being outdoors ——————————————

stroking a pet ——————————————

cooking ——————————————

woodworking ——————————————

reading ——————————————

engaging in hobbies ——————————————

socialising with friends ——————————————

journaling ——————————————

Amongst all these activities are two very easy, but often beneficial, strategies:

- deep breathing
- progressive muscle relaxation

## Deep Breathing

Deep breathing can be a wonderful way of relaxing and keeping a sense of 'calm'. It can also be very effective in helping with symptoms of anxiety. Best of all — it is completely FREE to do and we can basically do it anywhere and anytime!

There are a few different strategies used for deep breathing (including yoga breathing), however, I prefer the following:

1. Breathe in (inhale) through your nose to the count of 3 or 4 (so that would be 'one and two and three and four' as you breathe in).

2. You can choose to hold it there for a second if you wish, although this is not essential.

3. Breathe out (exhale) through your mouth gently to the same count — again, that would be 'one and two and three and four' as you exhale.

4. When you breathe in (inhale), make sure it is coming from your stomach/diaphragm as this enables oxygen to circulate to the brain (assisting with the brain functioning effectively). If you breathe from your chest (those short-shallow breaths we tend to take when we are stressed or anxious) this is similar to when we hyperventilate, and doesn't allow oxygen to flow to the brain properly, therefore the brain may not function effectively.

If you ever find yourself in a state of panic and unable to catch your breath during a panic attack or severe anxiety, one strategy that may help is to hold your breath for 1–2 seconds — this helps to reset your breathing and get it back under control.

## Progressive Muscle Relaxation

Progressive muscle relaxation is the process of progressively relaxing the muscles in our bodies. Please be mindful though that you should seek professional advice from your medical practitioner if you have any injuries to any area of your body, prior to doing progressive muscle relaxation.

Again, there are different ways that these can be done, however, I prefer the following:

1. Lie down (preferably — although it can be done in a seated position) in a comfortable position. Clench/tighten your feet as much as possible and hold for a couple of seconds. Then slowly release the tension.

2. Clench/tighten your calf muscles and hold for a couple of seconds. Then slowly release the tension.

3. Clench/tighten your upper legs and hold for a couple of seconds. Then slowly release the tension.

4. Repeat these steps using other parts of your body — example: buttocks, stomach, chest, shoulders, hands, mouth, nose, eyes, etc.

5. The process of clenching/tightening tightens the muscles but then relaxes the muscle when released. This can be an effective way of releasing built-up tension in our muscles. It can also help us to recognise when our body is tense vs relaxed.

# Module 5

# SMART Goal Setting

The idea of setting goals is to give us something to aim for, something we can accomplish. Goals can also help in providing us with a sense of direction. However, our goals need to be SMART for them to be more realistic and achievable. SMART goals also keep us accountable — if our goals are open-ended, they may never be achieved.

SMART stands for:

S pecific

M easurable

A chievable

R ealistic

T ime-based

Let's look at what each of these means in practice.

## Specific

What are you *specifically* hoping to achieve? For example — rather than 'I want to run a marathon', you would define this as something like 'I want to run in the 10km city-to-surf marathon next year'.

## Measurable

How will you measure your progress in achieving this goal? For example — by being able to run 1km each week for 2 months, and then increasing this to 2km each week, and so-on.

## Achievable

Your goals need to be achievable or they are unlikely to be met. For example — is running in a 10km marathon next July achievable for you because your level of fitness now is fairly good?

## Realistic

Are your goals realistic? For example — is it realistic to think that you could run 10km by July next year when you carry a longstanding knee injury?

## Time-based

Within what time frame do you want to achieve your goal? For example — July next year. Again, if this is open-ended (such as 'I want to run in a marathon'), it is unlikely to be achieved.

Of course, your goals don't have to be on such a grand scale as a marathon. You might have a couple of immediate very practical goals relating to work such as wanting to catch up on the monthly accounts of the practice or looking to instigate one of the time-management strategies we talked about earlier in Module 2. In any case, some goals may be ones that need to be done sooner than others. That's why the first step in goal setting is to break them down into short-, medium- and long-term goals.

## Short-term goals

Think about all the things you want to achieve within the next 3–6 months, and list them below. These are your short-term goals:

_____

_____

_____

_____

_____

_____

_____

_____

## Medium-term goals

Think about all the things you want to achieve within the next 6–12/24 months, and list them below. These are your medium-term goals:

_____

_____

_____

_____

_____

_____

_____

_____

## Long-term goals

Think about all the things you want to achieve within the next 1–2 years+, and list them below. These are your long-term goals:

_____

_____

_____

_____

_____

_____

_____

_____

For each goal that you identify you need to apply the SMART aspects to ensure you have the best chance of success in obtaining that goal. Setting up a goal worksheet will help identify the SMART elements of your goal. Ask yourself the following questions:

- What needs to happen to achieve each goal?

- How will you set about achieving these goals?

- What will it 'look' like when you achieve these goals?

- How will you 'feel' when you achieve these goals?

- How will you reward yourself for each milestone?

Complete your own worksheet based on the template above.

 **Sample goal worksheet**

On the opposite page is an example of a goal worksheet for a medium-term goal and a long-term goal. Try adding in the blank space one of your own goals to see if you can make it a SMART goal for you.

| Goal | S | M | A | R | T |
|---|---|---|---|---|---|
| | Specific | Measurable | Achievable | Realistic | Time based |
| | List specifics of your goal | How will you measure this? | Is this goal achievable? | Is this goal realistic? | What time frames? |
| Compete in Marathon | Run in Gold Coast 10km marathon | Engage personal trainer | Yes — if training regime is realistic | Yes — if stick to training regime | By July next year |
| Gain a Qualification | Diploma of XYZ | Research courses and enrol | Yes — I have the minimum entry requirements | Yes — I am capable of studying | Enrol by November this year |

# Module 6

# Acceptance and Commitment Therapy

I always like to provide a snapshot of what goes on in our minds, as a precursor to leading you through the strategies of acceptance and commitment therapy. Here are a few pointers I'd like to share with you.

Take a moment to think back to prehistoric times when our predecessors were out hunting and gathering. If they heard a sound, or saw a shadow, their minds likely would have perceived it as a threat — a predator coming to eat them (unless they were being mindful). They had to act quickly, and likely would have only had two options — stay and 'fight' for survival, or take off in 'flight' for survival (known as the 'fight-flight response').

Based on the fight-flight scenario above, our predecessors would have automatically assumed 'worst-case scenario' and acted on this (regardless of whether their perception of the threat was correct or not). So, the assumption would be along the lines of a predator being there to eat them. However, as we have evolved, our minds have much more to worry about than whether a predator is going to eat us! We have financial concerns, relationship concerns, work concerns, environmental concerns, and so on.

If you think about it, our minds are like storytelling machines — they are constantly describing to us what we perceive is happening. However, not all of these stories are helpful, and if we are not being mindful, we can easily get 'hooked' on unhelpful stories our minds are telling us. Before we know it, these thoughts are controlling our behaviour.

Our minds are also like problem-solving machines — they perceive a trigger (or threat, or problem), grasp on to it (or get 'attached' or 'fused' or 'hooked' to the thought), and then believe it without question (to put it another way, we 'buy into it'). If this thought is unhelpful (or unrealistic or not logical) and we act on it, chances are the response will be unhelpful or distressing in some way.

We cannot control our thoughts (that is, we cannot control what we will be thinking all the time). For example, we might not be thinking about a train, and it could be the furthest thing from our mind. However, if we suddenly see a train track and it reminds us of a past event when we were on a train our thoughts might then trigger a flow-on of memories and thoughts about that event. Now, all we can think about for the moment is that train trip. Similarly, if we try to control our thoughts by only thinking of something in particular for say five minutes, your mind is likely going to wander. Don't believe me? Try imagining that you are sitting on your favourite beach. Picture yourself there then focus only on that imagined experience for the next five minutes. What happened? Did your mind wander after only a minute or two? Were you perhaps thinking of how nice the beach is compared to another outdoor spot you like? Did you start remembering going to the beach as a child, or did you begin planning to go for a walk on the beach this weekend? For many of us, this process of focusing our mind is difficult as our thoughts tend to drift from that initial thought onto a host of different things. However, we can control what we do about our thoughts (i.e. our behaviour, and/or how we respond to those thoughts). Ideally, we would like our behaviour to be in line with our values to enhance our chances of wellbeing.

Another important thing to note is that our minds are also very powerful — they believe whatever they perceive! Don't believe me now either? Okay, here's another exercise to try. Think about watching your favourite television show or movie. As you are watching it, do you notice yourself laughing, crying, feeling tense, yelling at the screen, or some other response? Unless you are being mindful, your mind generally perceives what you are watching (or reading or listening to) as your reality, and responds accordingly. So, if you are watching something sad, unless you are being mindful, you might find yourself getting sad or crying — but the reality is that you are watching a television show that is not your reality at all (unless you are an actor or watching a home video!). Your mind perceives this as your reality and responds as if it were real.

You can also think of thoughts as boomerangs. They have a habit of coming back even though you discard them!

Some of the things you can do when you are having unhelpful thoughts (beyond the exercises we are about to look at here) are to try asking yourself — is there any evidence for this thought? Is it logical to have this thought? Is it realistic to have this thought? Is it helpful to have this thought? You can also ask yourself — does my worrying, crying, anger, happiness, etc. change the reality of the situation? The answer is most likely no, yet we continue to let these behaviours control us! In general, the thought is not so much the problem — it is our actions (or what we do about it, or how we respond to the thought) that is the problem.

Remember, just because we are thinking about it, doesn't mean it is true! And even if the thought IS true, it is our behaviour that will have the consequences. That is, we can have a thought and choose NOT TO act on it, which will result in a consequence. Or, we can have that same thought and choose TO act on it, which will result in a different consequence. Ideally, you want to pick the one that will give you the best consequence (or outcome) in the long run, aligned with your values.

### ☑ What are your values?

There is little point in learning about ACT without being able to put it into context and start using it. Therefore, these exercises are designed to help you identify your values and really put them into practice.

Firstly, make a brief list of all the things you value in your life, summarising them into each of the following core value areas. You will get more specific with them in the next few questions.

• Personal growth/health

_____

_____

_____

_____

• Work/study

_____

_____

_____

_____

• Relationships

_____


_____


_____


_____

• Leisure

_____


_____


_____


_____

Then make a list of all the values related to you personally, such as your health, religion, spirituality, etc. For example, these could include 'having time to meditate', 'exercising', 'eating healthy food', 'studying spiritual courses' etc.

_____


_____


_____

_____

Now make a list of your values related to work and/or study. For example, these could include things like 'working where I feel valued', 'working with colleagues who have a sense of humour', 'loyalty', 'feeling appreciated', etc.

_____

_____

_____

_____

Next you need to make a list of your relationship values. Break these down into the following relationship groups:

• Intimate relationships (that is, with a partner)

_____

_____

_____

_____

• Family relationships (that is, relationships with your immediate and extended family, excluding your partner)

_____

_____

_____

_____

• Social relationships (that is, relationships with other people who are not your partner or family — this could include work colleagues, friends, neighbours, club mates, etc.).

_____

_____

_____

_____

The final value list is your leisure time — this is how you choose to relax and unwind outside of work and/or study. For example, this could include things like gardening, socialising with friends, reading, art, surfing, walking, etc.

_____

_____

_____

_____

## What is ACT?

You will recall from Chapter 4 that acceptance and commitment therapy (pronounced as the word 'act' rather than 'A-C-T') aims to help people move forward in a way that is in line with their values. It helps people to become aware of their automatic reactions by assisting them to think and feel what they are physically thinking and feeling in that moment, rather than their assumption of what they are thinking and feeling.

Values are those things you want to stand for, the things that give you meaning and purpose. They are a little different to your morals, ethics, or standards, as those things tend to have rules attached to them — for example ... 'I must' or 'I have to' or 'I should'. In the context of ACT, values are actions, and you will learn more about how to use them throughout this module.

The ACT acronym stands for:

A = Accept your thoughts and feelings in the present moment.

C = Choose a direction you value to move yourself forward.

T = Take action toward that valued direction.

There are six core processes in ACT, which are designed to enable the ability to be more 'present' in the current moment and to change or continue with certain actions or behaviours.

As well as the six core processes used in ACT to increase and enable a person's psychological flexibility — *acceptance, cognitive defusion, being present, self as context, values,* and *committed action* — is the key component of mindfulness.

## Mindfulness in Action

Mindfulness is a process of awareness, rather than a cognitive or thought process — it is essentially about being in the 'here and now' or 'being in the moment'. According to Dr Russ Harris, mindfulness can be described as paying attention with openness, flexibility, and curiosity. He believes the process of mindfulness involves the following three factors:

- Paying attention, or bringing awareness to, your experiences in the present moment, rather than becoming caught up and 'buying into' your thoughts.

- Even though it may be unpleasant, painful, or uncomfortable, be open to your experiences in the here and now, rather than fighting, avoiding, or running away from those experiences.

- Broadening and consciously being able to focus and direct your attention to the different aspects of what you may be experiencing in that moment.

Right now, in this very moment, is the only moment you can respond or react to the thoughts and feelings you are having right now. Once they are gone, they are gone, and they are outside of your control as you cannot go back in time to change them. Similarly, if they haven't happened yet, then they are also outside of your control. When you are being mindful, you are dealing with things right here and now, and are not caught up in things from the past or future. So, when you realise you are in the present moment by being mindful, you can then take steps in line with your values to get better results in the long term — rather than just getting short-term gains.

There are many ways of practising mindfulness, and they don't have to be complex or confusing. One quick and easy technique is to *just notice*. That is, just notice five things you can see, hear, feel, taste, touch, and smell. This simple technique helps to bring you back into the current moment, which then enables you to take action so you can begin noticing your thoughts and feelings. Another easy technique is to simply be mindful by just sitting down somewhere quiet, and start focusing on your breathing. That is, just notice each breath as you inhale through your nose (to the count of three or four) and then exhale through the mouth (to the count of three or four).

It is quite normal for your mind to start to wander when you are trying to be mindful or meditate, so if this happens during this process, simply acknowledge those intruding thoughts by saying 'thank you', and then bring your attention back to your mindfulness activity.

## Acceptance

The stage of acceptance is considered the 'open up' stage. Acceptance means you can allow and make room for emotions that may be painful, or sensations, urges, or feelings — without struggling to try and change their form or frequency.

When you can accept things, it is not like you are accepting them as a welcome addition to your life; rather, it is an acknowledgement of the reality of the situation. It allows you to let these sensations, emotions, feelings, thoughts, and urges to just 'be', and lets you have room to breathe and stop struggling with them. It is not the same as acknowledging you like these things or are welcoming them, it simply means you are willing to make room for them.

## Cognitive defusion

Cognitive defusion is considered the 'watch your thoughts' step. This step is the process of being able to detach yourself from those memories, thoughts, feelings, and images, and separate yourself from them. Think of it like cars driving past you on the street — simply driving past you but you are not stopping to greet each car going past. Defusion is being able to allow your thoughts and feelings to come and go, instead of being pushed around by them.

You can also think of defusion as likened to the process of crossing the street. Imagine you want to cross the road, but on the way across the road there are people at either side of you stopping to chat. When you practice ACT, you are simply imagining crossing the road and acknowledging those people, however, you are not stopping to chat with each of them — your focus is on the end result of getting to the other side of the road, while still acknowledging the people along the way.

This stage allows you to notice your thoughts for what they are — they are simply just words or pictures, that aren't always true, real, or helpful!

## Being present

This stage is about being in the present moment, or the 'here and now'. Sometimes it can be difficult to be able to stay focused in the present moment, as we tend to catastrophise and worry about the future or get caught up ruminating in the past. When this happens, it results in us 'buying into' or becoming engrossed and absorbed in those thoughts.

At other times, we can start to act as if we are on 'automatic pilot' where, rather than being conscious and aware of our experiences, we simply just go through the motions — seemingly doing what we've always done, and then getting what we've always got.

When you are being present, it allows you to experience what is going on in that moment, rather than having those thoughts and feelings control your behaviour by responding on autopilot.

## Self as context

This stage of ACT can be described as the stage of 'pure awareness'. It can be a little difficult to understand this concept, as it refers to what is described as two elements of the mind that are quite distinct – the *observing self* and the *thinking self*.

The observing self is that part of you which is aware of what you are feeling, sensing, thinking, or doing. The thinking self is that part of you which is constantly thinking – it is thinking about beliefs, fantasies, memories, plans, judgements, etc. Most of us have an awareness of this part of ourselves.

When you think about how you have progressed through your life, you notice that your body changes, your feelings change, your thoughts change, and so forth. This is the observing part of you which is noticing or observing these things.

## Values

As mentioned earlier, your values are the things you want to stand for – those things that give you your sense of meaning and purpose. Values are also actions – so if, for example, you value being healthy, as an action you can choose to eat healthy foods, or exercise regularly, and so on. It is a choice you make in line with your values.

When you are living life consistently with your values, it feels balanced and content. When you aren't living your life in line with your values, it is unbalanced and does not feel 'right'. Think of your values as those things you really want, and when you get them, it feels good. Similarly, when you don't have them, it doesn't feel so good. Obviously, it is unrealistic to expect to live in line with your values

100% of the time. However, the closer you are to your values, the better it will feel.

Here's a quick exercise — think about a time when you felt really good about something that happened — now think about why that felt so good. This will tell you something about your values. Likewise, now think about a situation when you felt unhappy or discontent — now think about why that was so bad. This will indicate your values and how it feels less than desirable. It demonstrates that when you see or experience actions that go against your values, you feel 'bad'. This exercise is a useful way of really trying to break down your values and easily identify them.

## ☑ Rating your values

For this exercise, you will rate your list of values you made earlier in this module on a scale of 0 to 10 where:

0 = not living at all by my values
10 = living fully by my values.

When you think about your **personal growth/health values**, how close to living fully by your values would you say you were? What score would you rate this value, from 0 (not living by this value at all) through to 10 (living fully by this value)?

When you think about your **work/study values**, how close to living fully by your values would you say you were? What score would you rate this value, from 0 (not living by this value at all) through to 10 (living fully by this value)?

When you think about your **relationship values**, how close to living fully by your values would you say you were? What score would you rate this value, from 0 (not living by this value at all) through to 10 (living fully by this value)?

> When you think about your **leisure values,** how close to living fully by your values would you say you were? What score would you rate this value, from 0 (not living by this value at all) through to 10 (living fully by this value)?

## Committed action

The committed action stage is the final process in ACT and can be considered the 'do what it takes' stage whereby you take action, or behave, in a manner that is aligned with, or guided by, your values.

Taking committed action is the point where you need to take whatever action is needed to live in line with, or aligned to, your values — even though this may bring pain or discomfort. It is important to note that just because you live in line with your values, it does not always mean you will avoid unpleasant situations, which is unrealistic. What it does mean, however, is that in the long run, you will feel better for having acted in line with your values rather than acting against your values.

Whenever you are faced with a decision, you need to consider the long-term consequences from the action you will take, and not the short-term benefits. It is the long-term consequences with which you will have to live. For example — if you are thinking of drinking six glasses of wine because you want to avoid dealing with a difficult situation, in the short term this may feel good. However, in the long run the consequences are that the problems are still there after your drinking bout and you also have a hangover. You need to act on your values to get results — merely just thinking about them will not make the process work.

## Using Mindfulness

While there are many mindfulness strategies available, they do not need to be complex. One of the quickest and easiest ways to get in the moment and be mindful is to:

- Look around the area where you are right now, and notice or name 5–10 things you can physically see. Do not get caught up in what you can see, rather, simply just notice them — for example, you might see a window, plant, glass, computer, etc.

- Now repeat this process, but this time notice or name 5–10 things you can hear. For example, you might be able to hear the whirling of the ceiling fan, a clock ticking, other people talking, phones ringing, and birds chirping. Again, do not get caught up in analysing what you can hear — simply just notice them.

- If you need to, you can repeat this step, but take notice instead of what you can touch, taste, feel, and/or smell.

## Using Defusion

Following on from the mindfulness step, as you become aware of the things you can see, hear, feel, touch, etc., now bring your attention to what you are thinking and/or how you are feeling — right now, in the present moment. Do not 'buy into' these thoughts and feelings, or start analysing them or catastrophising about them, rather, just notice them for what they are — words your mind is telling you.

Now ask yourself 'are these thoughts/feelings helpful?' In other words, what you are asking is whether or not they are going to 'work' for you, or be beneficial for you in the long run, if you choose to believe them and act on them. Remember, one of the goals of ACT is for long-term benefit, not short-term gain.

If the thoughts/feelings are helpful, let them be (as they are not causing you any concern). If they are not helpful, you need to defuse (or detach) from them. This can be done in a few ways, such as saying:

- 'thank you thoughts/feelings for reminding me I am feeling ....' or

- 'thank you mind'.

The simple act of just acknowledging the thought/feeling allows you to detach from it.

## Taking Action

This final step requires you to be aware of your values — that is, the things that are important to you, and things you want to stand for — such as being honest, being kind, being calm, having good health, etc.

Think about the thoughts and feelings you have (or have had) that have been unhelpful or made you feel bad, and how you would normally automatically respond to them. Stop and ask yourself — does this help you and make you feel good in the long run? There is a fair chance they do not, which is a good indicator that those actions or behaviours are not consistent with your values. Instead of responding in the same 'auto-pilot' way you normally would, you now need to think of how you would ideally like to respond in order to receive long-term benefits. If this makes you feel better or somewhat better, it is indicative that it is aligned with your values.

☑ **Using your values to take action**

You identified your values and rated how they currently fit into your life earlier in this module — now it's time to take action! Look over your list and the scores you allotted to each entry.

The closer you are to a score of 10, the closer this indicates you are to living by your values (which generally equates to a sense of wellbeing in that area). The further away you are from a score of 10 (i.e. closer to 0), indicates you are not fully living by your values, and generally indicates you do not have a sense of wellbeing in that area.

As a starting point, you should aim to look at the value group with the lowest number and make a dedicated commitment to start changing. This means that the values you wrote down on your list are unlikely to be happening at the moment. Therefore you should start doing more of them and integrating them back into your daily life!

## A case example of how to use ACT

Imagine it is a really hectic day at the practice. You have had a number of walk-ins, as well as a high number of bookings. You have had to convey bad news to a family about their beloved family pet plus argue with another owner over the cost of surgery for their cat. You began your work day already under stress from difficulties at home. You numerous deadlines due at the same time, leaving you feeling very stressed and overwhelmed. Your thoughts might be telling you things like: 'This is too much — I will never get through all of this! I can't take it anymore!'.

Does this scenario sound familiar? Quite likely! So let's take a look at how you could use ACT in this situation.

### Step 1 — Mindfulness

First off, take a few deep breaths to calm down and get yourself grounded or centred, then bring your awareness to your thoughts and feelings. You might be feeling tense and anxious with a racing heart and thinking things such as 'I can't get out of this'. To deal with those thoughts and feelings use the strategies below:

- Visualise writing a thought/feeling on a leaf. Place the leaf on a stream and watch it float down the stream and away from you.

- Visualise writing the thought/feeling on a box. Place it on a moving conveyor belt and watch it move down the belt and fall off the end.

- Visualise the thought/feeling moving across a TV or computer screen.

- Name 5 things you can see, 5 things you can hear, and 5 things that have contact with your body now, for example, the trees outside the window, conversations in the waiting room, the feel of the bench on which you are resting your hand.

- Describe in as much detail as you can something in the room.

- Become mindful of your breathing. Notice the breath as it comes in and out through your nose, the rise and fall of your rib cage, and the rise and fall of your abdomen as the air fills and leaves your lungs.

### Step 2 — Example questions to ask yourself

Having identified specific thoughts, you need to assess the quality of these thoughts concerning where you are in the moment and how you can best help your mental wellbeing. Ask yourself:

- 'Is this a helpful thought?'

- 'Does it help me to take action to create the life that I want?'

- 'What would I get from buying into this thought?'

- 'What would happen if I allowed myself to get all caught up in this thought?'

- 'Does this thought help me in the long run?'

- 'How old is this story?'

- 'Who is driving the attention bus right now?'

If the thought is **not helpful,** try using a defusion statement and then a mindfulness strategy to help you refocus your attention. The aim is not to get rid of the thought but to simply let it be there in the background so that your time, energy and attention can be put to something more important.

## Step 3 — Example defusion statements

- 'Thank you mind for the thought that ...'

- 'I'm having the thought that ...'

- 'I'm having the thought that I am ....'

- 'I notice that I'm having the thought that...'

- 'Thank you mind for the X story ... I have read this story so many times before I don't need to read it now. I can just let it be there in the background.'

- Say the thought in your head using a silly voice (like Homer Simpson).

- Sing the thought to the tune of a song.

- Imagine your negative chatter is like a pop-up advertisement on the side of a webpage that you quickly ignore.

- Repeat the thought and speed it up or slow down it down.

## Step 4 — Taking action in line with your values

Now think about how you want to respond to this stressful working day and how you are feeling about it. If the reality is that you still have to do all these things, then remind yourself worrying and stressing about them will not help or change this. It will only take away more time and lessen your effectiveness. Additionally, feeling stressed and anxious at work (or home) is not likely something you value! So, think about how you can respond to your colleagues and clients in the practice in a calm, more relaxed manner (which you do value). Then think about ways you can problem-solve. Can you delegate? Is there a client you know well enough to ask if they are happy to wait a while longer while you attend to something urgent. Remind yourself of time-management strategies you will be able to use on some of those office tasks that will be left at the end of the day.

In the long run, when you respond calmly and rationally, it will be more beneficial than having responded in a stressed-out, anxious manner because this will only add to your negative feelings and over-whelm you.

# Module 7

# Positive Psychology

As a refresher from Chapter 3 on positive psychology (or if you have skipped that chapter and jumped straight into the strategies), I want to remind you what positive psychology is – and is not. It is not about positive thinking, and it does not assume all other psychology is 'negative'. It is a branch of applied psychology that essentially considers people's character strengths, and builds on those strengths to enhance a healthy and balanced lifestyle. Basically, it looks at what is 'right', as opposed to the traditional clinical approach that focuses on what is 'wrong' (with ourselves, our organisations, our environment, etc.).

From a theoretical perspective, positive psychology is the study of engagement, meaning, and positive emotion, and it also attempts to measure, classify, and build these three aspects of life – the three aspects that make sense out of the notion of happiness. Secondly, from a scientific perspective, positive psychology is rooted in empirical research and has been described as 'the scientific study of optimal human functioning that aims to discover the factors that allow individuals and communities to thrive'.

From a practical perspective positive psychology helps us focus on what makes life worth living and how we can live the good life. It uses five pillars (referred to as PERMA) and 24 character strengths linked to six human virtues. A summary table of these virtues was presented in Chapter 3 on page 51.

You can complete a free *character strengths questionnaire* to find out your character strengths online at:

http://positivepsychsolutions.pro.viasurvey.org

So let's take a quick trip through some of the elements of positive psychology that we can apply in our daily lives to help promote our wellbeing.

## Positive emotion

Positive emotions can be anything that makes you feel good — such as laughing, watching a good movie, reading a great book, going for a walk, sitting by the beach, talking with a friend, painting, relaxing, etc. They include things such as joy, contentment, gratitude, serenity, love, and so forth.

☑ **Positive emotion**

Aim to include positive emotions in your day-to-day life by undertaking activities that increase your likelihood of achieving these positive emotions. Perhaps this involves watching a funny movie, reading things that make you laugh, or going for a walk in nature or near the beach if these evoke positive emotions in you.

## Engagement

Engagement can include any activity that makes you feel completely engaged in it — it is similar to that feeling we get when we are engrossed in what we are doing. This is also known as 'flow', which is said to enhance wellbeing.

 **Engagement**

> Complete the character strengths questionnaire and aim to use your top five strengths in different ways, every day. I recommend starting with your top strength and really focussing on that for the first week, and then move to your second strength, and so on. Otherwise, it can become a little overwhelming trying to incorporate so many strengths at once!

## Relationships

Relationships can include any relationship — such as intimate relationships, family relationships, social relationships, work colleagues, neighbours, shop assistants, etc. We need positive relationships in our lives to contribute to our sense of wellbeing.

**Relationships**

> Try to ensure you have people around you where you feel you have a positive relationship with this/these person/people. Increase the time you spend with them to enhance these relationships and show gratitude for the people who you are in relationships with. My motto is 'quality over quantity'! Knowing you have at least one person who is there for you no matter what can be much more helpful than having lots of people who aren't there for you.

## Meaning

Meaning is analogous to our 'calling' or our 'purpose' in life. What do you want to achieve in your life? What are your meaning and purpose? One way that I find helpful when trying to ascertain what gives us our sense of meaning and purpose is to think of something we would do for free. Chances are, this could be an indication of something you are passionate about, and that is part of your meaning and purpose.

✅ **Meaning**

> Think about your meaning and purpose, and then try to work out ways in which you can set out to achieve this/these. Again, think about something you would do for free. Perhaps it is related to animals — are there things you could do that involve animals (outside of your job) that could help you achieve this? Perhaps it is giving free first aid classes to the local community, or helping an elderly neighbour with some yard chores. (I'm sure you get the idea!)

## Accomplishment

Accomplishment is the feeling we get when we have done something that we set out to achieve (like achieving a goal). However, we don't always need our accomplishments to be major events — even accomplishment in simple things such as getting the weekly restocking done, undertaking a professional development course, or doing the morning rounds of animals kept overnight.

✅ **Accomplishment**

> Think of things you would like to accomplish, and how you can go about accomplishing these. Don't forget to use the strategies from the chapter on SMART goal setting to help you define these and give yourself the best possible chance of achieving them!

## Flow

Flow is said to be an experience that is so enjoyable that you are motivated to keep returning to this state. The concept of 'flow' is described as a state of concentration and effortless enjoyment, and can be defined as the 'holistic sensation that people feel when they act with total involvement'. It indicates an engrossing and enjoyable activity that is worth doing for the optimal experience and its own sake, without consideration of extrinsic motivation.

There are said to be nine components of flow.

1. challenge-skill balance

2. merging of action and awareness

3. clarity of goals

4. unambiguous feedback

5. concentration on the task at hand

6. paradox of control

7. loss of self-consciousness

8. transformation of time

9. autotelic experience

It has been reported that while engaged in their best work, some highly creative artists and scholars have reported the experience of flow. During this state, the reward is the experience itself, and the person is seen to be functioning at his or her fullest capacity.

Similarly, it is believed the experience of flow occurs when an individual's skills are neither under-utilised nor overmatched to meet a given challenge, and there is a symbiotic relationship between challenges and the skills required in meeting those challenges. As this balance of skill and challenge is fragile, apathy, anxiety, or relaxation are likely to be experienced if it is disrupted.

Based on the above theory, for flow to occur, interest, concentration, and enjoyment in activities must be experienced simultaneously.

## Flourishing

Positive mental health or 'flourishing' has been described as a combination of social wellbeing and emotional wellbeing. It is also thought that the presence of life satisfaction and positive affect can be assessed by your emotional wellbeing. It is believed that positive psychologists have enhanced an understanding of the conditions, emotions, character, and institutions that enable people to flourish.

 **Three good things**

This activity can be used in a variety of ways. It is recommended however that you use it in the following order:
1. Three good things about yourself
2. Three good things you have done today
3. Three good things you have seen or heard about today

To start, record three good things about yourself on a daily basis (and only the good things, not the bad!), and repeat this process each day until you have run out of good things. Then go to step 2 and then step 3.

You can also use this exercise within your relationships, by getting each person to say three things they like, love, respect, or admire about the other person.

## Mindfulness

Mindfulness meditation involves attending to, without judgement, one's present experience. One advantage of practising mindfulness is that it can be practised anytime and anywhere, even at the same time as completing daily tasks.

Mindfulness has also been defined as a way of paying attention and consciously bringing awareness to experiences in the present moment without being judgemental about the experience. It is likened to being in the 'here and now'. The practices of mindfulness are congruent with much of the theory and practice that is prescribed in positive psychology, and as a result, a large amount of research has focused on evidence for the beneficial aspects of positive emotions within positive psychology and how this can be increased.

Subsequently, functioning well includes a sense of self-determination (such as an ability to make choices) or autonomy, self-efficacy, competence, resilience in the face of challenge, or adversity (including the management and awareness of feelings, thoughts, and positive relationships which encompass kindness and empathy).

## Gratitude

It's no secret that gratitude is very good for your health and wellbeing. By appreciating what you have and being grateful for these things makes you a happier person, with long-term benefits such as better health, higher levels of positive emotions, more success, and more meaningful relationships.

 **Gratitude**

Gratitude is about our ability to be grateful for the things we have (or have had), rather than focusing on all the things we don't have.

This activity can be used in two ways.

Write a gratitude letter to someone who has played an important part in your life, but who you feel you have never really thanked. Arrange to meet the person (without telling them about your gratitude letter) and then read them the letter!

Obviously, it may be difficult to meet with this person. Therefore a modification of the above is to write the gratitude letter, and then post or email it to them.

A separate gratitude activity is to write a list of all the things you are grateful for, and complete this on a daily basis into a gratitude journal, or place them into a gratitude jar which you can pull out whenever you need some inspiration or cheering up!

You can also try the following gratitude exercises:

- counting your blessings — such as identifying three good things on a daily basis

- creating a beautiful day — such as thinking about the type of day you would ideally choose, and try to enjoy that day when it comes
- learning to worry well — such as designating a certain period of the day specifically for worrying.

## Random acts of kindness

Kindness can be considered as the act of being considerate, respectful, caring, and showing charitable behaviour towards ourselves or other people. Kindness is also considered to be a virtue, which essentially means it is a positive quality which is morally good. When we are kind to someone (and feel good about it), our body releases endorphins (or 'happy chemicals'), which help us to feel good (similar to when we exercise). Practising random acts of kindness can enhance these positive feelings!

☑️ **Practising random acts of kindness**

> For this exercise, do something random (and kind!) for someone else — it may be something as simple as letting someone go before you in the queue at the supermarket, holding the door open for someone, smiling at someone, paying someone a compliment, bringing the neighbour's rubbish bin off the road, and so-on. These acts don't always have to cost money like paying for someone's coffee or paying a toll for the vehicle behind you.

## Optimism not pessimism

Hope and optimism are two of the character strengths of positive psychology. Research has also shown many health benefits of optimism and having an optimistic (rather than pessimistic) outlook. The good news is that according to Martin Seligman, optimism can be learned! (You can read more about this in his booked *Learned Optimism*.)

In a practical day-to-day application, when you find yourself thinking of a worst-case scenario, try thinking and focusing on the positives of the situation instead — the 'best case' scenario.

## Forgiveness

Holding on to grudges can maintain negative thoughts and behaviours — which cannot be changed or controlled! Why hold on to these negative aspects and make ourselves miserable? While you don't have to forget what has happened, practising forgiveness goes some way to helping us in moving forward in a positive manner.

Sometimes the actions of another person can be unforgivable. In these cases, you can forgive YOURSELF for putting yourself through unnecessary pain and suffering. When you feel like you cannot forgive someone else, you are essentially taking responsibility for their actions — and no-one is responsible for their actions except themselves.

## Savouring

When we savour the things we enjoy in life, it promotes a sense of wellbeing each time we remember these things. By savouring them, we are allowing ourselves to experience positive feelings time and again! Whenever you are engaged in a pleasurable or enjoyable activity, really try to adopt mindfulness and notice (and savour!) each and every moment.

### ☑️ The perfect day

Allow yourself to daydream and imagine the 'perfect day' — What would you be doing? Who would you be with? Where would you be?

This task does require you to be realistic (i.e. you need to have the capacity to undertake the activities), but once you have pictured your perfect day, set about making it happen!

## Coping strategies

It is important to develop appropriate and healthy coping strategies in order to deal with the ups and downs of everyday life — after all, our reaction to the crisis isn't going to change things. Rather, it just determines whether we feel good or bad about it!

If you don't already have effective strategies for coping, I suggest you re-read the chapter on acceptance and commitment therapy, as these strategies can assist you with providing evidence-based techniques for dealing with the unhelpful thoughts and feelings we all struggle with from time to time.

Australian Veterinary Association. (2013). *High rates of suicide among vets is concerning*. Retrieved from http://petpep.ava.com.au/13075

Australian Veterinary Association. (n.d.-a). *Telephone Counselling Service*. Retrieved from http://www.ava.com.au/veterinarians/centre-professional-success/my-success

Australian Veterinary Association. (n.d.-b). *What sort of person becomes a vet?* Retrieved from http://www.ava.com.au/node/1113

Bartram, D. J., & Baldwin, D. S. (2010). Veterinary surgeons and suicide: A structured review of possible influences on increased risk. *Veterinary Record, 166*, 388-397. doi:10.1136/vr.b4794

Bartram, D. J., & Boniwell, I. (2007, September 2007). The science of happiness: achieving sustained psychological wellbeing. In *Practice, 29*, 478-482.

Braun, V., & Clarke, V. (2006). Using thematic analysis in psychology. *Qualitative Research in Psychology, 3*, 77-101.

Brooks, R., & Goldstein, S. (2004). *The Power of Resilience*. United States of America: McGraw-Hill.

Centers for Disease Control and Prevention National Institute for Occupational Safety and Health. Compassion Fatigue Awareness Project. Retrieved from https://www.compassionfatigue.org/

Cornell College of Veterinary Medicine. (n.d.). DVM Admissions - *Statement of Essential Skills and Abilities*. Retrieved from http://vet.cornell.edu/admissions/essentialskills.cfm

Crawford, J. R., & Henry, J. D. (2003). The Depression Anxiety Stress Scales (DASS): Normative data and latent structure in a large non-clinical sample. *British Journal of Clinical Psychology, 42*(2), 111. Retrieved from

http://ezproxy.usq.edu.au/login?url=http://search.ebscohost.com/login.aspx?d
irect=true&db=pbh&AN=10100708&site=ehost-live

Crawford, J. R., & Henry, J. D. (2004). The Positive and Negative Affect Schedule (PANAS):Construct validity,measurement properties and normative data in a large non-clinical sample. *British Journal of Clinical Psychology, 43*(3), 245-265. Retrieved from http://ezproxy.usq.edu.au/login?url=http://search.ebscohost.com/login.aspx?d irect=true&db=pbh&AN=14933956&site=ehost-live

DeGioia, P., & Lau, E. (2011). *Veterinarians prone to suicide: fact or fiction?* Retrieved from http://news.vin.com/doc/?id=4887042. Retrieved 17 February 2015 http://news.vin.com/doc/?id=4887042

Dickinson, G. E., Roof, P. D., & Roof, K. W. (2011). A Survey of Veterinarians in the US: Euthanasia and Other End-of-Life Issues. *Anthrozoos, 24*(2), 167-174.

Fawcett, A. (2013). *Farewell, Caitlin.* The Veterinarian.

Fawcett, A. (2014). *Burnout and depression in the veterinary profession.* Retrieved from http://www.smallanimaltalk.com/2014/02/burnout-and-depression-in-veterinary.html

Fritschi, L., Morrison, D., Shirangi, A., & Day, L. (2009). Psychological wellbeing of Australian veterinarians. *Australian Veterinary journal, 87*(3).

Gable, S. L., & Haidt, J. (2005). What (and Why) is Positive Psychology? *Review of General Psychology, 9*(2), 103-110. doi:10.1037/1089-2680.9.2.103

Gardner, D. H., & Hini, D. (2006). Work-related stress in the veterinary profession in New Zealand. *New Zealand Veterinary Journal, 54*(3), 119-124. doi:10.1080/00480169.2006.36623

Harris, R. (2009). *ACT Made Simple — A quick start guide to ACT basics and beyond.* Oakland, CA: New Harbinger Publications, Inc.

Hatch, P. H., Winefield, H. R., Christie, B. A., & Lievaart, J. J. (2011). Workplace stress, mental health, and burnout of veterinarians in Australia. *Australian Veterinary Journal, 89*(11), 460-468. doi:10.1111/j.1751-0813.2011.00833.x

Hayes, S. C. (2004). Acceptance and Commitment Therapy, Relational Frame Theory, and the Third Wave of Behavioral and Cognitive Therapies. *Behavior Therapy, 35*, 639-665.

Hayes, S. C., Barnes-Holmes, D., & Roche, B. (2001). *Relational Frame Theory: A Precis.* Kluwer Academic Publishers, 160.

Hayes, S. C., Luoma, J. B., Bond, F. W., Masuda, A., & Lillis, J. (2006). Acceptance and Commitment Therapy: Model, processes and outcomes. *Behavior Research and Therapy, 44*, 1-25.

Hath, T. J. (2002). Longitudinal study of veterinarians from entry to the veterinary course to ten years after graduation: career paths. *Australian Veterinary journal, 80*(8), 468-473.

Heath, T. J. (2004). Recent Veterinary Graduates — Changes in veterinarians' initial career experiences over the last five decades: An abridged report. *Australian Veterinary Journal, 82*(10), 602-604.

Heppner, P. (1999). *Research design in counseling* (2nd ed. ed.). Belmont CA: Brooks/Cole Wadsworth.

Hoare, P., McIlveen, P., & Hamilton, N. (2012). Acceptance and commitment therapy (ACT) as a career counselling strategy. *International Journal for Educational and Vocational Guidance, 12*(3), 171-187. doi:10.1007/s10775-012-9224-9.

Interview participant five (2015, 22 January 2015). [Personal communication].

Interview participant four (2013, 15 August 2013). [Personal communication].

Interview participant one (2013, 21 August 2013). [Personal communication].

Interview participant six (2015, 22 January 2015). [Personal communication].

Interview participant three (2013, 22 August 2013). [Personal communication].

Interview participant two (2013, 28 August 2013). [Personal communication].

Johnstone, M. (2015). *The Big Little Book of Resilience.* New South Wales, Australia: Pan Macmillan Australia Pty Ltd.

Jones-Fairnie, H., Ferroni, P., Silburn, S., & Lawrence, D. (2008). Suicide in Australian veterinarians. *Australian Veterinary Journal, 86*(4).

Kahler, S. C. (2014). Moral stress the top trigger in veterinarians' compassion fatigue. *JAVMA News.*

King, J. (2009). *Riverside Girls High positively embracing positive psychology.* Paper presented at the First Australian Positive Psychology in Education Symposium Sydney, Australia.

Kinsella, M. (2006). Suicide in the veterinary profession: The hidden reality. *Irish Veterinary Journal, 59*(11).

LaFollette, A. M. (2010). The Values in Action Inventory of Strengths: A Test Summary and Critique. *Graduate Journal of Counseling Psychology, 2*(1).

Lees, J. (2014). *Secrets of Resilient People.* Great Britain: Hodder and Stoughton.

Linley, P. A., Joseph, S., & Boniwell, I. (2003). Positive Psychology — Fundamental Assumptions. T*he Psychologist, 16*(3), 126-143.

Lovibond, S. H., & Lovibond, P. F. (1995). *Manual for the Depression Anxiety Stress Scales*. (2nd. Ed.). Retrieved from http://www2.psy.unsw.edu.au/groups/dass/

Macwhirter, P. (2002). A life course approach to veterinary science. *Australian Veterinary Journal, 80*(8), 454-455.

Mann, J. J., Waternaux, C., Haas, G. L., & Malone, K. M. (1999). Toward a Clinical Model of Suicidal Behavior in Psychiatric Patients. *American Journal of Psychiatry, 156*(2), 181-189. doi:doi:10.1176/ajp.156.2.181

Martin, L. (2014). *WA mentoring program tackles high vet suicide rate*. Retrieved from http://www.abc.net.au/news/2014-06-07/suicide-rates-high-amongst-veterinarians.

Mellanby, R. J. (2013). *Improving wellbeing in the veterinary profession: Recent advances and future challenges*. Retrieved 16 February 2015, from group.bmj.com

Miller, A. (2008). A Critique of Positive Psychology — or 'The New Science of Happiness'. *Journal of Philosophy of Education, 42*(3-4), 591-608.

Peterson, C. (2006). *A Primer in Positive Psychology*. New York: Oxford University Press, Inc.

Peterson, C., & Seligman, M. (2004). *Character Strengths and Virtues. A handbook and classification*: Oxford University Press and American Psychological Association.

Peterson, C., & Seligman, M. (2005). *VIA Inventory of Strengths*. from Values in Action Institute.

Platt, B., Hawton, K., Simkin, S., & Mellanby, R. J. (2010a). Suicidal behaviour and psychosocial problems in veterinary surgeons: a systematic review. *Soc. Psyhiat Epideiol*. doi:10.1007/s00127-010-0328-6

Platt, B., Hawton, K., Simkin, S., & Mellanby, R. J. (2010b). Systematic review of the prevalance of suicide in veterinary surgeons. *Occupational Medicine*. doi:10.1093/occmed/kqq044

Popadiuk, N. E. (2013). Career counsellors and suicide risk assessment. *British Journal of Guidance & Counselling, 41*(4), 363-374. doi:10.1080/03069885.2012.726964

Rasmussen, J., & Robertson, G. (2014, 2014). [Personal Communication].

Savickas, M. L. (2005). *The theory and practice of career construction*. In S. D. Brown, & Lent, R. W. (Ed.), *Career development and counseling: Putting theory and research to work* (pp. 42-70). Hoboken, NJ: John Wiley & Sons.

Savickas, M. L. (2012). Life Design: A Paradigm for Career Intervention in the 21st Century. *Journal of Counseling & Development, 90*(1).

Savickas, M. L. (2013). *Career construction theory and practice.* In S. D. Brown, & Lent, R. W. (Ed.), Career development and counselling putting theory and research to work (2nd ed., pp. 147-183). Hoboken, NJ: Wiley.

Savickas, M. L. (n.d.). *Career Construction Theory.* Retrieved from www.vocopher.com/pdfs/careerconstruction.pdf

Savickas, M. L., & Porfeli, E. J. (2012). Career Adapt-Abilities Scale: Construction, reliability, and measurement equivalence across 13 countries. *Journal of Vocational Behaviour, 80*(3), 661-673. doi:10.1016/j.jvb.2012.01.011

Schulenberg, S. E., Strack, K. M., & Buchanan, E. M. (2011). The meaning in life questionnaire: psychometric properties with individuals with serious mental illness in an inpatient setting. *Journal of Clinical Psychology, 67*(12), 1210-1219. doi:10.1002/jclp.20841

Schull, D. N., Morton, J. M., Coleman, G. T., & Mills, P. C. (2012). Final-year student and employer views of essential personal, interpersonal and professional attributes for new veterinary science graduates. *Australian Veterinary Journal, 90*(3), 100-104. doi:10.1111/j.1751-0813.2011.00874.x

Schultz, K. (2008, May 2008). *An emerging occupational threat?* dvm Newsmagazine.

Scotch College. (2009). *Positive Education at Scotch College.* Paper presented at the First Australian Positive Psychology in Education Symposium Sydney, Australia.

Seligman, M. (2002). *Authentic Happiness.* Milsons Point, NSW Australia: Random House Australia.

Seligman, M. (2011). *Flourish: A visionary new understanding of happiness and well-being.* New York, USA: Free Press.

Seligman, M., & Csikszentmihalyi, M. (2000). Positive Psychology — An Introduction. *American Psychologist, 55*(1), 5-14.

Seligman, M., Ernst, R. M., Gillham, J., Reivich, K., & Linkins, M. (2009). Positive Education: Positive psychology and classroom interventions. *Oxford Review of Education, 35*(3), 293-311.

Seligman, M., Steen, T., Park, N., & Peterson, C. (2005). Positive Psychology Progress — Empirical Validation of Interventions. *American Psychologist, 60*(5), 410-421.

Shirangi, A., Fritschi, L., Holman, C. D., & Morrison, D. (2013). Mental health in female veterinarians: effects of working hours and having children. *Australian Veterinary Journal, 91*(4), 123-130. doi:10.1111/avj.12037

Sleeman, J., Booth, M., & Phillips, R. (2009). *From Strength to Strength: Developing a positive school philosophy at Hornsby Girls' High School.* Paper presented at the First Australian Positive Psychology in Education Symposium Sydney, Australia.

Steger, M. F., Frazier, P., Oishi, S., & Kaler, M. (2006). The Meaning in Life Questionnaire: Assessing the presence of and search for meaning in life. *Journal of Counseling Psychology, 53,* 80-93. Retrieved from https://www.authentichappiness.sas.upenn.edu/

Steinberg, S. B. (2007). *Positive psych*ology and schooling: An examination of optimism, hope, and academic achievement. (Doctor of Philosophy in Education Dissertation), University of California, Berkeley, United States. (UMI 3275612)

Teyler, H. (2013). *The thing I hate about being a veterinarian.* Retrieved from http://hstdvm.wordpress.com/2012/07/02/the-thing-i-hate-about-being-a-veterinarian

Tran, L., Crane, M. F., & Phillips, J. K. (2014). The Distinct Role of Performing Euthanasia on Depression and Suicide in Veterinarians. *Journal of Occupational Health Psychology, 19*(2), 123-132. doi:101037/a0035837

Tucker, R. P., Wingate, L. R., O'Keefe, V. M., Mills, A. C., Rasmussen, K., Davidson, C. L., & Grant, D. M. (2013). *Rumination and suicidal ideation: The moderating roles of hope and optimism.* Suicide Research: Selected Readings. Volume 10 - May 2013-October 2013. Brisbane: Australian Academic Press.

Tyssen, R., Hem, E., Vaglum, P., Grønvold, N. T., & Ekeberg, Ø. (2004). The process of suicidal planning among medical doctors: predictors in a longitudinal Norwegian sample. *Journal of Affective Disorders, 80*(2–3), 191-198. doi:http://dx.doi.org/10.1016/S0165-0327(03)00091-0

Tyssen, R., Vaglum, P., Grønvold, N. T., & Ekeberg, Ø. (2001a). Factors in medical school that predict postgraduate mental health problems in need of treatment. A nationwide and longitudinal study. *Medical Education, 35*(2), 110-120 111p. Retrieved from http://ezproxy.usq.edu.au/login?url=http://search.ebscohost.com/login.aspx?direct=true&db=c8h&AN=106094977&site=ehost-live

Tyssen, R., Vaglum, P., Grønvold, N. T., & Ekeberg, Ø. (2001b). Suicidal ideation among medical students and young physicians: a nationwide and prospective study of prevalence and predictors. *Journal of Affective Disorders, 64*(1), 69-79. doi:http://dx.doi.org/10.1016/S0165-0327(00)00205-6

Vetlife. (n.d.). *What factors cause stress in the veterinary profession?* Retrieved from www.vetlife.org.uk/personal-issues/stress-anxiety

Watson, D., Clark, L. A., & Tellegen, A. (1988). Development and validation of brief measures of positive and negative affect: The PANAS Scales. *Journal of*

*Personality and Social Psychology, 47,* 1063-1070. Retrieved from https://www.authentichappiness.sas.upenn.edu/

Webb, K. (2008). *The 8 Character Traits of Successful Veterinarians.* Retrieved from http://ezinearticles.com/?The-8-Character-Traits-of-Successful-Veterinarians&id=1503317

Whitcomb, R. (2010). Study looks at factors in high veterinary suicide rate in U.K. *DVM Newsmagazine.*

Wrzesniewski, A. (n.d.). *Work-life questionnaire.* Retrieved from www.authentichappiness.org

Wrzesniewski, A., McCauley, C., Rozin, P., & Schwartz, B. (1997). Jobs, Careers, and Callings: People's Relations to Their Work. *Journal of Research in Personality, 31*(1), 21-33. doi:http://dx.doi.org/10.1006/jrpe.1997.2162

CPSIA information can be obtained
at www.ICGtesting.com
Printed in the USA
BVHW041015060519
547457BV00021B/2185/P